A WELL CARED FOR HUMAN

SELF-LOVE STRATEGIES FOR TRANSFORMING YOUR PAIN INTO POWER

KORY M. SHRUM

TIMBERLANE PRESS

This book includes events that reflect the author's present recollections of experiences over time. Some names and characteristics have been changed to protect the identity of the person, and some dialogue has been recreated for the sake of clarity.

Although every precaution has been taken in preparation of the book, the publisher and the author assume no responsibility for errors or omissions, and hereby disclaims any liability to any party for any loss, damage, or disruption caused by errors or omissions, whether such errors or omissions result from negligence, accident, or any other cause.

No part of this book shall be reproduced or transmitted in any form or by any means, electronic or mechanical, or by any information storage or retrieval system without prior written permission of the publisher and author, except in the case of brief quotations, embodied in reviews and articles. Thank you for supporting the author's rights.

All rights reserved.
Copyright © 2024 by Kory M. Shrum
Editing by Toby Selwyn

ISBN: 978-1-949577-71-6

AN EXCLUSIVE OFFER FOR YOU

I have an additional ebook full of self-care strategies that you will receive for free if you sign up for my newsletter. I also send you other freebies from my catalog and host a monthly giveaway exclusive to subscribers. If exclusive stories and giveaways sound like something you're interested in, please sign up at www.awellcaredforhuman.com

Whether you come for the goodies and stay for the photos of my dog, in all cases, you are free to unsubscribe at any time.

Thanks!

Kory

For you.

For the you you were,
For the you you are,
For the you you are becoming.

A MOTHER'S MURDER, A DAUGHTER'S SALVATION

Triumphant stories are usually *only* triumphant because of their losses. Hardship always precedes the win. The low always comes before the high. Hope is lost before faith can be restored.

Otherwise, what is there to triumph over?

Most people assume my greatest loss came when my mother was murdered. And as heartbreaking as that experience was, that's not where my story begins.

But wait—isn't this supposed to be an inspirational book? A *motivational* book about how anything is possible?

Yes. That's certainly the goal.

Then why are we talking about loss and murdered mothers?

Because I want to show you how to leverage your losses. Not only how to navigate the heartbreak and fallout of life's challenges more easily but also how you can use the opening your loss created to transform your situation, your problems, and most importantly, yourself.

How does loss create an opening? Because it detaches us from that which we were previously bound: a person, a job, a place, a dream, a desperate desire.

We usually don't like this detachment. Not one bit. But that doesn't change the fact that once we are dislodged, we are now free to forge something new.

When my mother died, a door certainly slammed in my face. I had to say goodbye to a few dreams.

The dream that life would ever get better for her. The dream that things could get better between us, that it would be safe to see her more frequently, to spend more time with her. I imagined, often, the day when I was wealthy enough to buy her a house and the round-the-clock care and supervision she needed. When I'd finally have the means to get her away from her destructive family.

Fourteen years before a homicide detective called me to ask if my uncle had a history of violence against her, it was a hospital that had called to give me bad news.

"There's been an accident."

I was a student at the time, taking summer classes because I was trying to finish my graduate degree more quickly. I was also hoping to make up for the time I'd lost as a struggling undergraduate, trying to survive.

What had I been trying to survive?

The chaos of my family, certainly. My mother was diagnosed as bipolar. As a result, she was unpredictable. Her behavior was erratic and she would disappear altogether sometimes. She drank too much. Used drugs. There were her bouts in jail and the repetitious, heart-crushing news that some man had left her black and blue and bleeding on my grandmother's doorstep once again. Or that once re-welcomed inside, my uncle had continued where the other had left off.

Apart from my mother's self-destruction, I was also surviving the spinoff of my own traumatic childhood and all the bad habits it had created. I was too scared to get hooked on drugs and alcohol, though I'd done plenty of both. The real addiction in my teens and twenties had been codependent love affairs.

There was also the depression and anxiety so thick I would spend entire days in my bed or on the couch, forgetting to eat or drink. Or to even bathe.

Like many traumatized kids, I was also surviving the bondage of shame, half hanging myself with it on most days, a shame so lovingly nurtured by a narcissistic father until it was propagating like weeds in the garden in high July, no longer requiring any effort from him to grow.

I was surviving work stress, school stress, and little—or not so little—betrayals from so-called friends.

Not to mention all the torment of being on your own at twenty-three and having no idea what a quarterlife crisis is because you have, in fact, spent every single day of your life in crisis and you simply call this latest emergency *a Tuesday*.

By the time I reached graduate school, at least I knew I wanted to be a writer.

I had a dream. Something to focus on besides the hurricane in my head trying to unravel me from the inside out.

I was eating.

A lot of ice cream from the Dairy Queen next door to my duplex, granted, but I *was* eating.

I was starting to see progress. I was *just* starting to relax.

Until I got this call that my mother was dying in a hospital.

"There's been an accident. She's coming out of surgery now and we don't know if she'll make it. How soon can you come?"

I drove like a demon to Nashville, which was about an hour away from my school. I prayed the whole way there: *Please don't let her die, please don't let her die, please don't, please...* At the time, my relationship with God was about as healthy as my relationship with my mother, but old habits die hard.

By the time I arrived, she was out of surgery and they'd moved her to the ICU.

When I walked in, her room was dark, all the lights turned down low. Only the one behind her bed shone, backlighting her like a saint. Her bandaged head was wrapped up like a smashed thumb, beneath twenty layers of gauze.

There was a tube draining the blood away from her brain.

I looked at that tube for a long time, trying to make sense of it. I couldn't tell if the blood was coming or going.

My mother was awake but she couldn't speak. She couldn't answer the typical questions like "Who is the president? Do you know what month it is? Do you know who this is?"

When the nurse pointed to me, my mother only smiled.

Afterward, the doctor pulled me aside.

"What happened to her?" I had a lot of guesses, none of them great. Maybe it was another boyfriend or girlfriend that left her like this. Maybe she'd drank too much, or had been too high and had gotten behind the wheel of a car. Or maybe she'd been perfectly sober but her dark mind had said, *Drive right into that concrete barrier there, Leitha,* and she had.

Sometimes my mother listened to such voices.

I remember how tired the doctor looked, the puffiness of his dark eyes. "We only have what the police report says, and the eyewitness testimony, but it seems like your uncle struck her so hard in the head with something, it actually broke her skull."

I would find out later that it requires hundreds of pounds of force to break a skull. My uncle somehow accomplished this with a glass ashtray.

The doctor went on. "We were able to do the surgery and repair the damage. We put a steel plate in her head. But as you can see, she's going to need to go to a rehabilitation facility after this in order to relearn how to walk, how to talk, and regain the functionality she's lost due to the brain injury."

I burst into tears at some point. I felt bad about that.

Tears didn't stop me from initiating strategy mode. Before the good doctor even finished explaining the situation, I'd begun mapping a path toward resolution, seeking a viable way forward, turning the problem over in my mind like a puzzle box meant to be solved.

This incident—the phone call, the bad news, the dropping everything and rushing to her side—had triggered a long-ingrained pattern in me. What I call "savior mode."

That constant fear for her safety and the crushing weight that somehow it was my responsibility to keep her safe was familiar. I'd carried that belief close to my heart since I was a little girl.

Beliefs reinforced every time I stepped between my mother and whoever her assailant was, when I hid her keys or her pills. I'd invented so many little versions of the *keep Mommy safe* game.

And not just her physical safety either.

I considered her emotional well-being and her happiness my responsibility too.

If I found her crying, or if I knew she was sad, I always tried to cheer her up. But it was a lot of work for a child. Given that she was bipolar, her moods were frequently unstable.

So when the doctor sat across from me in a sterile room and told me what he thought had happened and what needed to happen next, I did what I'd always done.

I left the hospital that night and immediately began rearranging my life so that I could take care of her. It didn't matter that having my mother come and live with me didn't make any sense, financially or otherwise.

I was compelled by my one overwhelming desire: to keep my mother safe.

I asked my roommate to move out so I could have the spare room (a terrible financial decision). I asked my professors to work with me on deadlines (how quickly I forgot my academic priorities), and I asked my job to be flexible in my scheduling (I was almost fired for this).

I tried to get friends to agree to check on her when I was at work or school, because now I had a new fear that with her brain injury she might get confused and wander out into traffic and get hit by a car. Maybe she'd even be lured by the very enticing light of the Dairy Queen sign, as I so often was.

I was trying to find a bed for her, curtains. Drawers for her clothes. When I went to the store to buy myself stuff—shampoo, conditioner, food—I started making decisions based on her preferences. *Maybe she'll like this. Oh, she'll hate that.*

I wanted her to feel welcome.

More importantly, I had *plans*.

Plans for how this time would be different. This time was my big chance to get my mother out of my grandmother's house, where she'd been living with her violent brother before the accident, away from the drinking, the drugs. This would be the fresh start and new life I'd always wanted for her.

I got carried away with dreams of what our relationship could be like, if she just got better. That maybe, just maybe, this brain injury would prove to be a blessing in disguise.

We'd have the relationship I'd always wanted.

A safe one. A stable one. One in which she was the mother and I got to be the child.

I was already fully committed to these delusions by the time a second phone call came a few weeks later.

This one was from the rehabilitation clinic she'd been moved into after leaving the hospital. She was supposed to stay for a minimum of six weeks in the facility, relearning how to walk, how to talk. At six weeks they were going to reassess her progress and see if she needed a longer stay. By then I hoped to have my place sorted so she didn't have to go back to my grandmother's even for a single night.

But it had not yet been six weeks when a very distressed woman from the facility called, apologizing as if she'd accidentally set my mother on fire.

"She's gone," she said. "She had some guests, and when we went to check on her, she was *gone*. She took off her wrist band and slipped out against medical advice."

In a perfectly normal, perfectly calm voice, I thanked the woman for calling in.

I waited until after we said our goodbyes to panic.

I called everyone I could think of. I drove back to Nashville and checked all the places she could've possibly been—bars, dealers, friends. I couldn't find her.

Do you know where she was?

Do you know *where* I found her finally, once the panic wore off and I began to think clearly?

You might think I'm stupid when I tell you.

After all, it would have made sense to call my grandmother's house first. She *had* been living there at the time of the accident. And it's where my uncle had caved in her skull and almost killed her weeks before.

So why *hadn't* I checked there first?

Because I had believed her.

Every day that I had visited my mother in the rehabilitation clinic, I'd sat with her and made plans with her about how our lives would be once she came home with me.

We'd spent hours of each visit making these plans.

I had believed her when she'd said, "Of course I don't want to go back to Nana's. Of course I don't want to be in the same house with that bastard. I only stay here because I have nowhere else to go."

"But now you do," I'd told her.

"Now I do," she'd agreed.

Except she'd escaped the facility and returned to my grandmother's house. She'd abandoned her treatment halfway through just to go back there. My uncle, the most violent and dangerous of my mother's abusers, had been waiting for her, ready to offer his usual pathetic run of halfhearted apologies.

You might think that finding my mother back at my grandmother's house just weeks after she'd almost died should've been enough for me to give up on my mom, but it wasn't.

Back then I had a much higher tolerance for misery.

Now, not so much.

Instead, I drove over there and called her from the end of the driveway because I wouldn't even go into the house. Not with him there. My uncle had assaulted me once, on the day of my grandfather's funeral. He'd reached out to choke me, had missed and broken my sunglasses across the bridge of my nose. I ran to a neighbor's house—they called the police, and off to jail he went.

I never set foot in my grandmother's house again.

I do learn some lessons more quickly than others.

From the driveway, with my mother on the phone, I said, "If you still want to get out of here, if you want somewhere else to go, I'll take you with me now. You can *still* come live with me. Isn't that what you want?"

"Yes," she said again. "I just had nowhere else to go."

As she slid into the passenger seat with her shaved head, all sixty-four staples in the shape of a question mark visible on the side of her skull, I remembered how I'd shaved off the last of her beautiful hair in the bathroom adjacent to her little rehab suite. How she'd cried even though she was the one who'd asked me to do it.

And now here she was, bald, with that terrifying line of pinched skin, but at least she was in my car and not in that house with him.

"Can we make one stop before we get on the highway?" she asked.

I assumed that she needed cigarettes. She'd been a smoker all my life. She'd loved to tell the story about the only time she'd quit was when she was pregnant with me.

"When you came out, the nurse asked if I wanted to breastfeed, and I said hell no! Give me a damn cigarette. But it was worth it, baby, because look at you. You're perfect."

I stopped at the nearest gas station, and Mom went in. Only she didn't come out with cigarettes. She came out with beer.

This was a problem.

This was a problem for *so* many reasons.

Did she forget about the medication she was supposed to be taking for her injured brain? Did she forget about her failing liver, thanks to the hepatitis C she'd contracted from intravenous drug use?

It wasn't even about the promise she'd made to me at the rehab. "Of course I'll quit drinking. I haven't even wanted a drink since I woke up from surgery. This is the fresh start I've prayed for."

It was the fact that I had one objective: to keep her safe.

And when my mother drank, that was impossible to do. When she drank, her behavior was unpredictable, often putting her in physically dangerous situations. When she drank, she was emotionally unstable, making it harder to soothe her.

I was wrestling with my lifelong desire to keep her safe, and here she was sitting next to me in my car with sixty-four staples punched into the side of her head, opening a beer while looking me dead in the eyes.

In this moment, I was confronted with the possibility that the person hurting my mother most in the world was herself. And how do we protect someone from themselves?

We can't.

And I'll say it again, louder for those of you in the back.

It *can't* be done.

We can't protect people from themselves. This truth is one of the most painful I've ever had to accept.

"If you drink that beer it's going to kill you," I said.

"Don't be so dramatic," she said, and opened the beer. "This won't last me two days."

She started to drink it.

And here it is. The pivotal moment. My chance to make a decision that would change everything.

Until that moment, I'd believed that if I just tried hard enough, sacrificed enough, did enough, planned enough, fought enough—*was* enough—I could *make* my mother safe. That I could get the relationship I wanted with her.

I'm willful and I'm stubborn and more than a little idealistic, but everyone has a limit.

Here, I'd found mine.

Watching her open that beer so close on the heels of her brush with death incinerated my delusions.

Loss can do that.

It was abundantly clear that my options were to stay in the codependent dance with her, trying to achieve the impossible—force salvation upon her—or I could choose to break the cycle.

I could choose, for the first time in my life, to save the only person I actually could.

Myself.

And that's what I did.

In my sweltering, beat-up clunker of a car, with less than twenty dollars to my name, that's what I chose.

Me.

I drove my mother right back to my grandmother's house and I left her there at the end of the driveway. Then I threw the car into reverse and drove back to the life I was desperately, and very imperfectly, trying to build.

I had wanted to weave my mother into the fabric of my new life but could now see that was never going to happen.

That dream was slipping like sand through my fingers as I drove away despite the crushing fear that I was leaving her to die.

I knew that if I left her there, in *that* house, with *that* man, it was only a matter of time before he killed her. After all, he'd come so close this time.

And then what happened?

Fourteen years later, almost to the day, I got a phone call from a homicide detective, telling me that he was arresting my uncle. That he believed my uncle was responsible for my mother's death.

Do I even need to tell you that I blamed myself?

Do I even need to speak of the guilt that threatened to consume me whole?

I shared the story of her death, the investigation, and the family secrets uncovered in the wake of that experience in *Who Killed My Mother?*, first as a podcast, then as a book. So I won't do it again here.

But what I will say is that my mother's death was a great loss.

And as with every loss, I was cracked wide open. All the hope poured out, and after it did so, new paths and possibilities were born of my grief.

You already know what your losses are.

Like me, I'm sure you carry them quite close to your chest.

We're here now to talk about what you can do next. When these openings present themselves, you have options, choices, for how you want to leverage all that loss and heartache.

So no, this book isn't about loss. Not really.

I will share my losses for one reason and one reason only: to prove that it can get bad—as bad as it can possibly get—and you can still set yourself free.

This *is* a book about triumph. And a path we can take to get there.

Everyone's path is different, of course. But if we're lucky (and we are), this book will serve as a field guide to your well-being. If nothing else, I hope it will be a bit of comfort on an especially cold and unforgiving day.

If you're ready, please allow me to show you where the path back to yourself begins.

. . .

Key Chapter Takeaways

- We cannot save someone from themselves. No matter how much we love them.
- As terrible as loss is, it will always create openings and new possibilities.
- These openings are precious opportunities for transformation. It's our choice how to make the most of them.
- No matter what has happened to us, no matter how tragic, we can always find our way back to ourselves.

BEATING THE ODDS

Sometimes the only way out is through. In therapy we call this processing.

And I processed my mother's death the way I process everything: creatively. Creativity is a powerful healing tool that has served me well over the years. It's brought me more peace, strength, and understanding than I ever imagined possible.

No surprise then that within five months of her death, I'd launched my first podcast: the *Who Killed My Mother?* show. I wrote the music for it using a steel-tongued drum that my wife had given me for a previous anniversary. My friends called the simple little tune "hauntingly beautiful."

Perfect.

I was certainly haunted by my own guilt and grief at the time.

On the show, I told stories about my mother, what it was like growing up with her and my family. And I shared the details of her death and the investigation. This went on for a year, this chronicling of the events following her death, and me offering up the evidence, the autopsy report, the secrets and revelations to strangers on the internet. Eventually I put it all together in a memoir and published it with the same title.

This was how I coped. It was how I made sense of everything.

But my grief still crept into my fiction projects too. I'd been writing *The City Below* when my mother died. A story set five hundred years in the future. What was meant to be a fun, pithy little sci-fi tale with mystery elements became something else. My police commander heroine, Grace, lost her husband and son in an explosion meant to kill her. She became racked with guilt and threw herself into her work to atone for it.

Sound familiar?

Eventually Grace moved on. She found love again and got revenge on the murderous bastard who killed her family.

And I, too, came out the other side of my sorrow.

By the two-year anniversary of my mother's death, a lot had changed.

I'd finished *Who Killed My Mother?* My uncle was dead—and no, I wasn't responsible for his passing, as tempting as it may have been. And I'd stopped talking to my narcissistic father.

I'd also come to understand I wasn't the same person I'd been when it had all started.

Or rather, I saw myself quite differently.

Because that's the trick of transformation. Sometimes it isn't some great personality change. Someone doesn't necessarily come in and rearrange the furniture of your life, your mind.

Often it's simply that someone turns on the light and you finally get a good look at the dark room you've been shuffling around in for the last decade. All those sharp edges you've been bumping into suddenly have names: triggers. Though who the hell arranged the furniture like that: poor coping skills. And why has no one paid the light bill: generational trauma.

Or perhaps someone polished the mirror you've been using all this time and you finally get a good clear look at your features without all those distortions from the smudges and warped glass.

In both cases, everything changes in the same instance that nothing changes at all. The mind dilates and your thoughts flatten out into one giant, *Ohhhhhh*.

That was me.

During that time of the investigation, I learned of my mother's detonation event, as I'd come to think of it. The horrific experiences that shattered her young mind when she was a child. I now understood my mother in a way I never had.

Her death also offered me the chance to understand myself. To look at my life and see what had changed over the years. Because while it was true that one phone call from a homicide detective had brought me to my knees, crying, begging, and praying for my mother's forgiveness, it was equally true that my life at thirty-seven looked *very* different than my life had at twenty-three.

"And thank the Lord for that," as my mother would have said.

I believe I've painted my life at twenty-three pretty clearly for you in the introduction: chronically lovesick, depressed, anxious, codependent, self-destructive, suicidal, and with disordered eating no less. There had been lots of lying motionless in the dark staring at the ceiling. Days and days of it.

By thirty-seven, I had become the full-time author I'd always dreamed of being. I hadn't escaped my student loans yet. Those were still a blight on my existence. But financial difficulties—and some chronic back pain—were about the only complaints I had. I was brushing my teeth every day. I was in a loving marriage. I had my own home. It was safe, charming even. I had an office full of books, and a thousand little half-completed passion projects. There was a birdfeeder outside my office window. And while it's true it pissed me off when the squirrels swung upside down from it shamelessly dumping all the seeds on the ground, there were still plenty of birds to be had.

I was still eating ice cream, lots, but I was no longer crying while I did so. Nine out of ten times anyway.

All of which is to say that my life had become quite beautiful. Somehow, despite the odds.

The only problem was I hadn't realized it yet.

What they don't tell you about trauma is that you may very well be long out of the war zone before *you* consider the war over.

I was still running around the battlefield of my mind the day the detective called me.

I was running more slowly, true, but only because I was growing very, *very* tired of running.

My mother's death forced me to stop, if only because I suddenly had a compelling question pinning me in place.

What had changed?

In my life. In me.

Everything, it had seemed.

But my mother's life had stayed on the same trajectory. Her death was proof of that. What I had most feared would happen fourteen years before had, in fact, happened. Meanwhile I could hardly believe the life I'd built. It was part of the reason I struggled so much with enjoying it.

I wasn't so naïve as to believe this improved life was simply because of a few choices I'd made. I am a hard worker. True. But we both know that countless people work very hard every day of their lives to make good choices and still life gives them nothing but bad breaks.

So why were things getting better for me?

I had to know.

If I couldn't answer that question, I would start running again. Running because that's what you do when you don't feel safe enough to stay put. It feels impossible to relax into the blessings of your life, when you believe, as you've been conditioned to believe, that the next great catastrophe is overdue.

It'll show up any day now, and when it does, we will call this one a Wednesday.

My paranoia about whether or not I was actually okay only intensified after concluding *Who Killed My Mother?* I received a lot of emails from people thanking me for that show (how lovely) but also asking me how in the world I was such a healthy, well-adjusted person after everything that had happened in my life.

I was very tempted to write back and remind them that it's important not to believe everything we see or hear on the internet. But I was too busy interrogating myself. Asking myself the same questions.

Am I okay? Really? Are we sure? How do we know?

It wasn't long before I wanted answers even more badly than they did.

In this quest to reassure myself, I came across a study called ACEs. The Adverse Childhood Experiences survey. In this study, the Center for Disease Control looked at the effects of childhood trauma specifically. Their focus was on events that undermine our sense of well-being as a child. Every child needs to feel safe and loved. Certain events—death, divorce, violence, alcohol and drug use, incarceration, abandonment, mental illness—cut right through our sense of safety and belonging as children.

The more of these harmful events we experience, the higher our ACEs score.

I took the quiz and got a score of eight out of ten. Ten points is the most traumatized, according to their scale. I also took the quiz as my mother—using the information I'd learned about her while writing *Who Killed My Mother?*—and she also had a score of eight.

You can find out how traumatized you were as a child by taking the ACEs quiz [1] in case you're looking for something fun to do on Friday night.

Invite your friends over. Have a fight about who is *really* more scarred. What could possibly go wrong?

Most people (about sixty percent) have at least one ACE, but things don't look good for you, statistically, if you have four or more. With four or more ACEs, your risk for negative health outcomes sharply rises. For example, you're 1,220% more likely to attempt suicide, 1,003% more likely to use injected drugs, 460% more likely to have recent depression, [2] and 230% more likely to have hepatitis.[3]

Reading the descriptions of how ACEs affect our well-being as adults felt like reading a textbook description of my mother and her struggles.

She first tried to commit suicide when she was twelve years old, to escape the sexual abuse she was enduring. She didn't escape it. As she got older, her mental health only grew worse. She was put on medication, which didn't mix well with the drugs and alcohol she was using to self-medicate. She contracted hepatitis from a dirty needle. She struggled to hold down a job and didn't have a single healthy relationship in her adult life.

As rough as life had been for me in the beginning, by my late thirties my situation was quite different. I no longer wanted to unalive myself, first and foremost.

That was helpful.

I overcame my eating disorder. I was rarely depressed. I still struggled with anxiety, especially in respect to my finances, but it was manageable. My relationships had evolved from codependent dramas reminiscent of daytime soap operas to shockingly healthy and supportive bonds.

Statistically, my life should look like my mother's. We have the same family dynamics and similar trauma records. But mine had gone in a completely different direction.

Why?

I set off to answer that question in my second podcast, *A Well Cared For Human*. And while writing those weekly episodes about how to take good care of yourself, I identified pretty quickly what had changed.

Those fourteen years between when I'd left my mother at the end of the driveway and when the homicide detective called, giving me the worst news of my life, made all the difference.

What had happened in those years? I built a healthy relationship with myself.

This relationship is what my mother never achieved.

This positive self-relationship was the secret ingredient that transformed my life.

It saved my life.

And I hope it will save yours too.

Key Chapter Takeaways

- The ACEs survey examines the effects of childhood trauma on adults.
- If you have an ACEs score of four or more, then you are at a higher risk for negative health outcomes like suicide, drug use, depression, anxiety, chronic pain, or hepatitis.

- It can take time to feel safe in your own life, even if you leave dangerous situations behind.
- The key to well-being is building a healthy relationship with yourself.

FOUR ATTRIBUTES OF A HEALTHY RELATIONSHIP

A healthy relationship consists of four components: honesty, trust, respect, and open communication. The more honesty, trust, respect, and communication shared between you and someone else, the stronger and healthier that relationship. But what about our relationship with ourselves? How can these four components be applied to self-love?

Honesty

When it comes to your relationship with yourself, honesty is about being honest with, you guessed it, *yourself*. You don't lie to yourself about where you are emotionally. You don't lie to yourself about your addictions or your sticking points. You don't lie to yourself and say it's perfectly *fine* that this person keeps mistreating you, or that it's totally okay that this job is sucking your soul from your body through a bendy straw. You don't lie to yourself about who you are, where you are, and what you need.

Many of us lie to ourselves, though. Often and with strong conviction. Why?

Two reasons.

First, because the truth is so terrifying. Leaving that soul-sucking job and putting your finances at risk is *horrifying*. Saying goodbye to your abusive family and striking out on your own feels like the ultimate betrayal. Just ask Rapunzel when she climbed out of the tower her narcissistic "mother" had her locked up in "for her own good."

Doing what we know is right for ourselves often runs counter to all the unspoken rules of families and culture and even reason. It's easier to tell ourselves lies and go with the flow than fight upstream against the current.

The second reason we lie to ourselves is often due to a lack of self-awareness. Self-awareness is a skill. When you're in survival mode or crisis, absolutely zero energy can be dedicated to developing self-awareness.

Many of us, when we are in survival mode, don't stop and think. We *can't* stop and think. A drunk uncle is throwing a bottle of beer at our head. An abusive father is pulling off his belt. A mother is drunk, belligerent, and looking for her car keys.

At times like these, thinking is a luxury we can't afford. We can't just sit back and consider, *Oh, I wonder what happened to this person when they were a child that made them the way they are today? And how might their current actions be shaping me in this very moment? Maybe if I just take a moment to think about this...*

No. That's a recipe for getting hurt.

Self-awareness is a powerful tool, but it needs time and space to develop, and destructive environments offer neither.

For me, honesty was only possible after I broke out of the toxic cycle with my family. It was hard to go against the expectation of, *But they're your parents. You only have one set of parents, and they just want what's best for you.*

Rejecting the idea that someone had the right to mistreat me just because they were family was the critical first step toward honesty for me. Admitting to myself that no, in fact, I wasn't okay with it.

Once I removed myself from the toxic environment, I had room to consider what was really going on beneath all my reactivity.

And I shut down completely.

I didn't like what I saw. The feelings I'd been running from were overwhelming, exhausting. I started going to therapy so that I would have a professional on my side who could help me sort through this mess I'd inherited.

In therapy I was forced to be honest too.

I was sitting on Dr. A's couch, in his dimly lit office. My eyes were so swollen from crying they were practically pinched shut. It had felt like all I did was cry in this man's presence, and I could not be more embarrassed by it.

I don't remember which awful experience we were unpacking that day, but what I do remember clearly is what he said to me when I'd finished talking.

He looked into my puffy eyes, and with a very loving, compassionate tone, he said, "Kory, I'm going to need you to say what happened to you was bad."

Immediately, I rejected the idea.

"I don't know. Was it? So many people in the world have it worse and—"

"Say it." His voice was firm but gentle. "Say it was terrible."

"I—"

"Say it was wrong. Say it was horrible. *Say* it shouldn't have happened to you."

I didn't want to. I didn't want to, in part, because then I'd have to admit that the people who were supposed to love and take care of me hadn't—and I was never going to get what was "owed" to me as a child—love, safety, and support. I was also resisting the admission due to my father's programming.

Often when he was abusive, and if I was brave enough to tell him not to hurt me, he would respond with, "You don't know how good you have it. You don't know what terrible is. You don't know how hard things can really be, and when I was your age, I had to shine shoes just so I'd have enough to eat, hoping that when I was done the drunks would actually pay me rather than kick me in the teeth. So don't tell *me* it hurts. You don't even know what pain is."

And I believed him.

I believed him, and yet I still had all this heartbreak that was eating me alive from the inside out.

"Say it, Kory," Dr. A urged. "You can't heal this unless you can first admit that there's a wound."

"It was terrible." I said it in a sarcastic tone. I said it with a half-shrug. Here I was trying to make a joke out of it, which was another way of turning away from my pain. "It was the absolute *worst*."

Then I burst into tears. Who knew you could burst into tears while already crying?

"Say it again," he said softly.

"It was hard," I said, and this felt very honest.

"Too hard," Dr. A said, with a kind smile. "Those things should have never happened to you. Kids aren't meant to experience stuff like that. But you did."

"But I did," I said. And the tears continued.

It was Dr. A's job to point out the truth. I just didn't like it.

That's the thing about honesty.

It can be shocking. Or at the very least unpleasant. It can be painful. It can be like opening a puss-filled wound.

Even when we start digging around in our heads and our hearts and we find good things to appreciate ourselves, we don't always like that either.

When I started to get to know myself, I saw my strength. My drive. My will. My independent nature. A strategic mind. Courage. All that creativity. But before I could get too proud of myself for these attributes, I had to acknowledge *why* I had these traits.

I was strong because people had repeatedly preyed upon my weakness. And because I was the only one who could protect me from those predators. I was brave because I was always in dangerous situations.

I was willful in order to defend myself from my father's repeated attempts to break me. I was independent because I'd been abandoned. My mind had been conditioned to be strategic because I'd spent the first twenty-five years in a maze of treachery and deception where the people I loved the most could pop out of a dark corner at any time and plunge a dagger into my chest. Strategy is a good skill to have when your childhood is a minefield. And creativity is honed when resources are scarce. When there's a lack.

All those losses had created opportunities to grow, but that didn't mean I had to be *happy* about it.

Not when it was so easy to feel resentful. To feel like maybe everyone else had gotten a better deal. Why couldn't I have been taught to be brave and strategic and creative *without* the trauma?

Surely it could be done. And to this day I maintain that it can be.

It's only that my family hadn't had the capacity.

And before you ask, no. My difficult experiences didn't turn me into a little rainbow-sunshine example of a human being with lots of character.

Those experiences gave me negative traits as well. Let's call these shadow traits.

Like any dog that has been kicked more than a few times, I could be snappish. I growled too quickly and too often. I could be suspicious of kindness. I rejected many lovely things that came my way because I didn't trust them. I was tired of being disappointed. I could be heavy-handed and dismissive of others trying to find the quickest path to a goal. Gentle wasn't in my vocabulary because no one had been gentle with me. And if they had tried, my first question would certainly have been "What do you want from me?"

But being honest with myself required that I look at all of it: the good and the bad. The positive traits and the shadows. What I liked and what I didn't.

By doing so, I was building awareness. Awareness allows us to be free of our programming.

When we aren't honest with ourselves, when we haven't taken inventory, we continue to act from a reactive place, from a place of survival. We aren't entirely in control of ourselves in this space because it's the animal in us that makes sure we survive.

I love animals, don't get me wrong. But I saw a video of an orca flipping a dolphin up into the air for fun the other day, and so I don't want my inner orca to be making decisions for me. She's a little unhinged, if I'm being honest. No one should leave her in charge.

But in charge she would be, as long as I remained unaware of my thoughts and actions.

And self-awareness has many other functions, not just in helping us to understand ourselves and what we're working with.

Any map we want to create for ourselves or our lives requires two points. We have to know where we want to go and we have to know where we are. Only then can we draw a path between those two points.

Honesty is about creating that map. Knowing who you are now, taking stock of the good and shadow traits and the issues at hand. That's one point on the map. Then being honest about what you really want for your life and for yourself regardless of everyone's expectations, that's the second point. You'll never get anywhere if you can't put those two points on your map.

You don't have to love where you are now.

In fact, you might actually hate where you are, perhaps even who you are, when you draw your little starting point.

You might even be wondering how the hell you ended up in this bog cesspool in the first place. What asshole abandoned you here in this seventh circle of Hell? You can figure this out along the way, but be forewarned, sometimes honesty reveals that the asshole was you all along.

Insert Unmasking the Villain Gasp while Taylor Swift's "Anti-Hero" plays in the background

But that's okay. You can work with that. You just need enough self-awareness to get your two points down on the map for now. That's our first step for getting out of Hell.

And drawing our two points begins with honesty.

Trust

Trust is the firm belief in the reliability, truth, ability, or strength of someone or something. If we trust someone, it's because we feel we know them. We know what they will and won't do. Perhaps most importantly, we are trusting that they won't hurt us.

Having the same level of trust and certainty about ourselves is difficult. Many of us would struggle to proudly declare, "I have no self-doubt. I absolutely and completely believe in myself and my abilities."

But once we've used honesty to put our two dots on the map, then we need to trust ourselves enough to undertake the journey from point A to point B.

It can also be hard to trust ourselves because often we receive feedback from others that creates this doubt.

In my case, self-doubt was cultivated by a narcissistic parent. Many narcissistic parents rely on a tactic called gaslighting in order to manipulate and control their children. Gaslighting is "an extremely effective form of emotional abuse that causes a victim to question their own feelings, instincts, and sanity."[4]

This destructive power dynamic is more detrimental in the parent-child relationship because in that relationship, society rules in favor of the parent. Children are expected to be obedient. They're not allowed to question a parent's motives or mistreatment.

More dangerously, a child's love is a pure love. I loved my father with my whole heart. When he came home from prison, I thought he would be my white knight, a savior riding into the whirlwind that was my mother's instability, and that he'd make good on all those promises of love and safety described in his letters during his years away.

I was ready to give just about anything to have his love and the dream life he'd painted.

Even without the complication of a child's blind adoration amplifying the effects of emotional and narcissistic abuse, there are severe side effects of gaslighting.

Anxiety, depression, post-traumatic stress disorder, and difficulty regulating emotions.

For me, the most debilitating symptom was the self-doubt, as it kept me from believing I had the power to help myself.

Due to the narcissistic wounding, I felt that my instincts and intuition couldn't be trusted. My own feelings couldn't be trusted. When I would speak up for myself or say what I knew to be true, such as "You're hurting me," he would then convince me that I had brought this on myself. "It's because you're weak like your mother. Crazy like your mother. You don't even know what's best for you. You don't even know how good you have it."

But you don't have to have the experience of narcissistic abuse to develop self-doubt. Many negative experiences can plant the seeds of self-doubt.

Any negative feedback or criticism from others can create that feeling. As children we will internalize that message of incompetence and feel like we're incapable of exerting power over ourselves and our environments.

When self-doubt is magnified to its most extreme version of itself, we get learned helplessness, as was the case with my mother.

As a child she was repeatedly exposed to the same gut-wrenching situation over and over again—a sexually abusive father and a mother who silenced her—until she began to believe she could never escape. She'd carried that belief into her adulthood, and that belief controlled her for the rest of her life.

If you struggle with self-doubt, you may feel as though you have a very good reason to doubt yourself. Maybe you made the worst mistake imaginable.

Maybe you even have proof that you have failed spectacularly. But learning to believe in yourself and your own power is a crucial element of having a great relationship with yourself.

If you got it wrong once or twice or two thousand times, it certainly doesn't mean that you can't get ever get it right.

Many of us have made big mistakes. I have certainly done things I am not proud of, things I wish I could take back. But you can learn to forgive yourself for the mistakes you've made and move past them if you're willing to process your regrets.

Everyone is out here making mistakes.

You're entitled to yours.

Even the spectacular ones.

What I want you to hear most here is that no matter what you have done, you can learn to trust yourself again.

As for myself, when I'm in a situation that calls for trust, I tell myself this: I may not get it right, but I'll do my best and with good intentions. If I fail, I can try again. If I hurt someone, I can apologize and mean it. I will always do better the next time, because I always learn with each attempt.

A little plan like this may encourage you to move forward as well.

Respect

There are two ways that respect applies to our relationship with ourselves. The first and most direct way is that you love yourself too much to hurt yourself. The second is that you respect your needs.

Not hurting myself—or others, for that matter—was something I had to get good at with practice. I had to unlearn the habit of self-harm.

For a long time I was a self-destructive person. I hurt myself because I did not love myself. Principally it was my body that I hurt. I hurt it or let other people hurt it.

I treated my body like an afterthought as I struggled with anorexia and bulimia, in turn starving and stuffing myself until I felt sick. I let others mistreat me in relationships. I had no boundaries, emotionally, physically, or otherwise.

As a child my thoughts, feelings, needs, and wants had never been respected by those around me. As a young adult, I felt I didn't even have the right to ask that I be treated well. One of my father's favorite phrases was "Respect is earned, not given." It's an odd motto to use with one's own child.

Self-respect is to love yourself so completely that you are proud of who you are.

You can even go so far as to admire yourself, believe it or not.

We can't expect others to admire us for who we are, though it's certainly nice when they do.

But we can expect them to respect our needs.

Bodies should be respected. Emotions should be respected though not necessarily indulged. Thoughts and desires can also be respected—as long as they're not used as a weapon to hurt others.

Respect is often a choice. I had to wake up one day and say, "I'm going to love myself too much to hurt myself." Then I had to wake up the next day and say it again because I didn't really believe it the first time, or the second, or the hundredth. Respect is a commitment that one makes continuously because challenges to that respect will always come, and we have to affirm again and again and *again* what we will and won't accept.

Boundaries are a big part of respect, and I have a lot to say later about boundaries.

For now, know that boundaries are multifaceted. You need boundaries internally to protect yourself from your own self-destructive tendencies: negative thoughts and self-loathing. You also need boundaries externally, a code of conduct outlining what others are and aren't allowed to do to you.

Boundaries don't have to be harsh or aggressive.

In the beginning, they were for me because I expected to have my needs violated by others as they had been all my life. I can't recall a single time when my parents or other members of my family ever respected a boundary.

For that reason, anytime I needed to enforce a boundary as an adult, I did so in full combat mode, in anticipation of the disrespect.

As a result, people found me blunt and abrasive. I didn't always handle things *diplomatically*.

I don't recommend this tactic, but if it's where you have to start, by all means please do. It is better to be a living bitch than a dead sweetheart.

But give your forcefulness a visa, not permanent residency. Not only because I wish everyone was kinder and gentler in this world—what a beautiful accomplishment that would be—but because forcefulness comes from a place of stress, tension, and hypervigilance that we're trying to outgrow along with all the other poor coping strategies.

For those of us that struggle with boundaries and saying no, I promise that with time and patience we can learn to enforce boundaries with more ease. I'm much more deft at setting boundaries now, to the point that sometimes people don't even realize they're playing by the rules.

Let's not get ahead of ourselves though. It's better to start wherever you are now and do whatever you can manage in this moment than spend another moment tolerating disrespect—from yourself or anyone else.

Ideally, in your relationship with yourself, you'd not only love yourself too much to intentionally hurt yourself, you'd also admire the hell out of yourself.

For many of us, however, we will see tremendous progress if we can just learn how to stop saying yes to shit we don't want to do. When we say no when we want to say no, we are respecting our time and our energy.

That alone is an impressive accomplishment.

Open Communication

Like respect, open communication has layers. One layer is deeply connected to respect as it involves enforcing boundaries. Learning how to tell others what I needed was an important part of honoring my relationship with myself.

I find it easy to speak up for others, especially someone I love. Perhaps it will always be easier to point at a spouse, a child, friends, even strangers, and declare, "Hey! She needs...", "Wait! He needs...", or "My friend would like..."

It's always been much harder for me to speak up for myself.

But communicating our needs and wants to others is an act of self-love. Just as you might speak up for someone you care about, you must learn to also speak up for yourself.

Considering how often my father liked to accuse me of selfishness and how often my mother's dramas consumed all the breathable air in the room, I didn't feel like I was allowed to have needs for the first couple of decades of my life.

It took me a while to figure out what I needed before I could even learn how to articulate those needs to others.

When I was about eleven years old, I went to the store with my father. He was looking for something he needed for work. Let's say it was a type of drill bit, though I have long forgotten what the item actually was. We were in the drill bit aisle and my father was looking at all the different options for length and thread, etc., when I realized I needed to go to the bathroom.

"Dad—"

"Not now." He cut me off. "I'm trying to figure this out."

His focus was on the drill bits, trying to puzzle out what he needed, what would get the job done.

"But—"

"Not *now*," he said. "You don't listen for shit, do you?"

Fine. I could see the bathroom sign at the end of the aisle. I'd just take myself.

Except I only managed one step before he grabbed my arm and wrenched me to his side.

"Where are you going?"

"To the bathroom!" I cried, trying to pull my throbbing arm away.

He only twisted it harder. "No, you're not. Stand here and be quiet. I'm almost done."

I needed to pee, my arm hurt, and he was not almost done. Once he got the drill bits sorted, he dragged me to another aisle, and another, and another, as he finished his shopping.

I had no choice but to stay with him.

We actually made it through checkout and to the front of the store when I hit my limit.

I pissed myself in the little alcove between the store's entrance and the parking lot.

I knew it was happening. I felt it coming on and had no power to stop it. I froze. Terrified. Embarrassed.

The piss ran down my legs all the same.

Because I'd stopped walking, frozen in place in terror, he turned back to see what the problem was. He swore when he saw my light blue overalls soaked through.

"What the hell, Kory. You're not a fucking baby."

I started to cry, which only seemed to increase his disgust and embarrassment.

"I tried to tell you," I said.

"No, you didn't. Don't try to blame this on me. Act your age."

This is what it can look like when someone is not allowed to communicate their needs.

Although my mother certainly wouldn't have done something like this, intentionally, I was often forced to put my needs to the side in favor of hers.

Her moods dictated the course of a day. If not her moods, then my pointless attempts to moderate her erratic behavior.

But this sort of need suppression doesn't exist only in abusive situations.

Many of us deny our need for sleep, for food, for water, for rest, for love, for comfort, for safety, for affection. Habitually, we suppress that little voice every time it speaks up.

I'm hungry—
I can't eat, I'm late.
I'm tired—
It doesn't matter. I have so much to do.
I want to feel safe—
But we can't leave her.
I need to rest—
But I can't. I'm too stressed.

We shush ourselves a thousand ways until that little voice gets so quiet we can't hear it anymore. Then we have to work really hard to turn up its volume. Often because by then, the volume on everything else (anxiety, fear, panic, overwhelm, heartbreak, you name it) is so much louder because those are the voices we've practiced listening to.

Abusive relationships can teach us to stop listening to ourselves. But so can demanding jobs, difficult circumstances, societal, cultural, or religious expectations. It is quite the process learning how to listen to yourself again. If there is a lot of self-doubt, it's even harder still because our first instinct is not to trust what we feel, nor to trust that little voice.

This is what communication with yourself is all about.

Open communication is about learning to listen to what you need. The obvious needs like a violent urge to use the bathroom, but subtle needs as well.

This isn't the right job for me.

I really shouldn't be her friend anymore. She only makes me feel bad about myself.

I want to start dating, even though my friends tell me it's not worth it.

I'm not ready for kids, but my family is pressuring me.

I don't want to drink this alcohol but everyone else is.

Open communication is also about learning to speak up for yourself even when it can be scary or risky to do so.

It's all four of these attributes together—honesty, trust, respect, and open communication—that help to develop our relationship with ourselves. There is quite a bit of overlap between the four attributes. The more we trust and respect ourselves, the more likely we are to speak up for ourselves and communicate our needs. The more honest we are with ourselves, the better we are at listening to ourselves, identifying those needs, and the more we respect ourselves, too.

So don't be too attached to the idea of *this is honesty* and *this is trust* and *this is*—

Focus more on anything and everything you can do to hone these skills, in whatever form or opportunity they may present themselves.

They really will get easier to wield the more you get comfortable using them.

And how do you get more comfortable with respecting yourself, openly communicating with yourself, trusting yourself, and being honest with yourself?

Practice, baby.

Keep practicing.

If you keep practicing, then it becomes only a matter of time.

Key Chapter Takeaways

- There are four characteristics of a healthy relationship with yourself: honesty, trust, respect, and open communication.
- Honesty is difficult because you may not like what you see. Look anyway.

- Honesty is the starting point for any life path change. You can't chart a change in course unless you know where you are now.
- Self-doubt negatively affects your relationship with yourself. But you can learn to trust yourself no matter what has happened in the past.
- Respect is about boundaries. You need loving boundaries with others, but also with yourself.
- Open communication is about learning to listen to yourself, but also about having the courage to speak up and advocate for yourself as your needs arise.

THE FOUR PILLARS

As I write this, self-care has become a rather hot topic. It's not difficult to find advice on how to best take care of yourself. This advice usually sounds like this: sleep more, eat better, get some exercise, get fresh air, stay off your phone, and touch some grass.

This is all great advice.

However, I have found it to be more helpful to think of my well-being as a relationship with myself rather than a list of boxes I need to check off.

A relationship is fluid. It has to be built and maintained. Sometimes it's strong and we feel indestructible. Other times it's shaky and needs more care and attention.

Checkboxes just don't convey the same level of depth and complexity.

The good news is that we can build and maintain this relationship. Before I tell you how, let me ask this:

If you were to rate your relationship with yourself today, what kind of score would you give it?

Is it great? Or at least *mostly* okay? Maybe a smidge bruised? Or has it just walked away from a ten-car pileup unsure how it's still alive?

Perhaps your relationship with yourself feels more like it's in a twenty-year coma and may never wake again. Or perhaps before now, you'd never even considered your well-being as a relationship?

Whatever the state of your relationship with yourself now, great, oblivious, or in the gutter, self-care practices are the tools we use to build and maintain that relationship.

However, if those tools are to be of any use to us, we have to know the condition of the relationship first and also what capacity we have for investing in the relationship.

If you're currently in burnout, for example, you don't have much capacity. All your circuits are fried. The gas tank is empty. Same for depression. There's only going to be so much you can do in a day before you're exhausted again.

Let's say I have a box of adhesive bandages. It might even be the *fancy* box of bandages with the different sizes, but it's still a box of bandages. And bandages won't work for every medical emergency.

For cuts and scrapes? Sure. Have a bandage.

But if someone offered you a bandage to cover your chest full of bullet wounds while you're still bleeding all over yourself, your prognosis won't be so good. And this is my issue with most self-care advice.

It doesn't account for the personal nature of self-care. Even if we were both going through a divorce and the conditions of these divorces were perfectly identical—we lived in the same neighborhood, made the same amount of money, we were the same race, we identified as the same gender, and we had the same reason for divorce—our individual experiences could still be miles apart.

Maybe your divorce provided a deep sense of relief and the freedom you've been longing for. Meanwhile mine triggered long-ingrained feelings of abandonment and not being lovable, tied to my personal history of abuse. You responded by making plans to move to Provence and run a bed and breakfast on a lavender farm.

I became a depressed little hermit who's had nothing but takeout all week.

This example is to illustrate that even in the exact same situation, people react differently and will need different things. That's what makes self-care hard.

It's one of the many reasons my mother never got better. She was offered a lot of bandages when what she needed was a whole triage team to sew her back together again.

I won't rant here about the failings of the American health care system or our nonexistent mental health care system. For now.

I'll only say that in order to address the very personal nature of self-care, it will be more helpful for me to outline the four pillars of your well-being.

Once you are made aware of these four pillars of your relationship with yourself, you will know where you can apply all that honesty, trust, respect, and open communication we just talked about.

You'll also have a better sense of how to choose self-care tasks that will be most helpful to *you*.

This way, you will have the power to build a strong relationship with yourself that will be flexible enough to serve you no matter where you are in your life now.

Hopefully this will help with discouragement too.

Often we give up on building our relationship with ourselves too soon because we listened to the bad bandage advice, saw no results, and spiraled into hopelessness.

So many of us work hard to make time for self-care, we even do the self-care, but still wonder why we don't feel better after weeks, months, or possibly years of investment.

Often it's because all that effort is being invested in the wrong place.

Someone once told me, "Kory, you just need to relax. Run a hot bath and climb in the tub with some wine and a good book. You'll feel *so* much better."

Telling someone with my family history to get drunk in the tub is not great self-care advice. It might be fun, but it's not going to improve my relationship with myself. Not only because of my family history of alcoholism, but because wine is also one of my migraine triggers.

And if I wake up with a migraine the day after, it's going to feel pretty hard to love myself and muster up some admiration for my *great* self-care efforts.

So let's begin with a blueprint. I'll walk you through building your own four-pillared wellness temple. Then you get to pick where the furniture goes. The decor. The corpses of your enemies. The coffee machine. Whatever you need, love.

Me: system.

You: details.

Got it?

Why can't I just tell you which self-care practices to do?

Because only you will know what's best for *you*.

The Pillars—And Why I Call Them That

I want you to imagine a Grecian temple. One of the old ones like the Parthenon, except that yours is much smaller. This temple of yours has four pillars holding up that heavy roof.

The first pillar is your body pillar. This pillar represents your relationship with your body. How you feel about it, think about it, speak about it.

The second pillar is your mind & emotions pillar. I put mind, which we can also call thoughts, and emotions together because they often co-arise. They are deeply entwined.

How often have you had an experience where your mind starts thinking up wild scenarios and you found that your emotions were all too willing to spiral into a panic along with the thoughts? And the reverse is true as well.

You may wake up with a sense of unease or depression, and your mind gets right to work on creating reasons for why you feel the way you do. Maybe it decides to remind you of the really embarrassing thing that happened twenty years ago, just because it's trying to match your energy.

So helpful.

Thoughts and feelings often feed and shape each other, so I honor that by letting them share a pillar.

The third pillar represents your relationship with your spirit. Spirit is a vague word that encapsulates many things. Do you have a great relationship with joy, creativity, playfulness, curiosity, spirituality, and awe? Or are you suspicious of every single ounce of happiness that flows your way? When someone acts too happy around you, does your lip curl up in disdain before you crab-scuttle off into the dark, hoping to wait it out until all the good feelings are gone?

If you are a religious or spiritual person, this pillar is also where your relationship with God or the universe would reside.

The fourth pillar represents your relationship with connection. I used to call this pillar *others*, but that wasn't quite right. *Others* implies that the focus is on other people. That what *they* think or say or do matters.

It doesn't.

Connection is a better word because it allows us to talk about the importance of building healthy, loving relationships with others, but it also allows you to look at your relationship with connection itself.

How comfortable are you with vulnerability? With opening up? How safe do you feel putting yourself out there and meeting other people? Can you share your feelings, your thoughts, or your ideas without fear of judgment or ridicule or criticism?

Oof. Not me. At least not all the time.

But having a good relationship with vulnerability is a powerful tool in our well-being toolkit. This pillar is also home to our boundary work.

These are the four pillars, the four areas of well-being: body, mind & emotions, spirit, and connection.

If your pillars are strong enough, they can take quite a bit of damage and still stand. They can even survive a bombing like the real Parthenon did in 1687, when a shootout between some Ottomans and Venetians caused heavy damage. Yet look at her now. Over three hundred years later and still harassed by adoring tourists daily.

No matter how many times this relationship with yourself collapses to complete and total ruin, you will always have the power to rebuild.

It's not always fun, but it can always be done.

Collapse is less likely the more pillars you have up and functional. Distributing the hefty weight of living across multiple areas of your life will make it all feel a lot lighter and more manageable.

It will be harder for a bad experience to knock you off balance if you have at least two or three pillars in working order.

That said, don't be discouraged if you don't have a single pillar to your name today.

For a long time, I didn't either.

In fact, allow me to show you just how bad things can get before they get better.

The Body Pillar

I don't know when I began to hate my body. But I do know that I was quite young.

It started with my legs.

My grandfather used to yell at me to straighten my feet when I walked. My father too: "Just put one foot in front of the other. Pretend you're walking on a straight line."

I couldn't really see my legs when I walked, so I didn't know what they meant. I did know I was pigeon-toed. If I looked down, I could see that my toes turned inward toward each other as if they were gossiping.

My grandmother mentioned that at one point they'd considered putting braces on my legs to straighten them, but cost had been an issue.

One day I was standing on my grandmother's patio. It was summer. I was wearing shorts and eating a popsicle. I'm not sure my age, but I couldn't have been more than ten.

My uncle (yes, the one who killed my mother) whistled, long and low, and said, "Look at those legs. They go all the way up to your ass."

In hindsight this comment makes no sense whatsoever. As far as I'm aware, everyone's legs—if they have legs—go up to their ass. But the bigger issue was the sexual undertone and menace behind the words.

Then I went to summer camp and a boy, surrounded by his jeering friends, pushed me down and called me bow-legged. He did this even though my arm was sprained and in a sling.

Soon after I stopped wearing shorts. I no longer wanted anyone to see my legs. And I didn't start wearing them again until I was in my thirties.

There was also the matter of my teeth. After I lost my front teeth, my permanent incisors grew in. Only these were adult-sized, and as a result they gave me a rather rabbity appearance. My chubby cheeks didn't help.

"You'll grow into them," my mother said. Fortunately, she was mostly right.

But not before my father complained about how crooked they were, how discolored, how imperfect. He wanted me to get braces, but I never did.

If not the legs or the teeth, there always seemed to be some new issue with my body. Some new problem.

In high school a boy said he didn't want to kiss me because my lips were too thin.

Another boy called my eyebrows over-tweezed. To be fair, this is accurate. No one tells you that if you try to give yourself Christina Aguilera or Gwen Stefani eyebrows circa 1999, there's a possibility that you'll damage the hair follicles and the hairs won't ever grow back.

Bullying aside, my father was the most consistent critic of my appearance.

"You have too much acne. Do you even know how to use a washrag? You're gaining weight. Exercise more. You have the worst posture. Sit up straight."

He made these comments right up until I saw him for the last time.

I was thirty years old.

The people in my life had taught me to dislike my body long before I even knew how I felt in it. This created a disconnect with my ability to be vulnerable in my body. It also made it hard to be honest with it. I was too busy trying to fix everything, to react to each new blow of criticism rather than take a close look at what I really thought and felt and why.

This also affected my respect toward my body. When you spend years hearing about everything that's wrong with you, it's natural to devalue your body too. By the time I was a teenager, my love and respect for my body was nonexistent. This disrespect grew to such proportions that I began cutting myself in my teens.

This is not uncommon. As much as 17 percent of teens[5] will self-harm. This act of self-harm is usually tied to a struggle to regulate emotions.

There was also the matter of my addiction to dramatic, codependent love affairs.

When I left Tennessee and got away from the pool of exes I'd collected, I promised myself that I would end this pattern.

In order to do so, I took a vow of celibacy. Before you get any ideas, this was not a religious or puritanical decision. I simply didn't trust myself to keep my own needs in the picture while also infatuated with someone. My needs were the first thing I yeeted out the window when I wanted to sleep with someone. I was trying to heal this compulsion by looking for ways to bond with people that weren't based on sex.

It was the worst.

Zero out of ten. Do not recommend.

I'm kidding!

But I did react the way many people do when they're trying to break a pattern of addiction: I replaced one bad habit with another.

In my case, I developed an eating disorder.

Eating disorders are often about control.

I was trying to gain control of my life. Of me. Of something. Anything.

Anything at all that would make me feel safe.

What is ironic about this is that when I was struggling with bulimia, I was very much out of control. I would walk into grocery stores and often find the bakery section near the front. That first scent of sugar was enough to trigger my desire to binge. I would buy donuts, cake, whatever I wasn't allowed to have but wanted, and rush home to gorge myself on it.

Before throwing it all up so it wouldn't "count."

It felt like the ultimate rebellion. Like I was somehow cheating the oppressive system I'd found myself in.

Then, while trying to heal bulimia, I swung to the other extreme: anorexia. My mind began playing all sorts of games to make eating okay. An unspoken checklist for when I was and wasn't allowed to eat.

If I didn't eat all day, then I'd earned an evening meal. If I had so much as a granola bar, though, that meal was forfeit. Or if I spent a couple hours in the gym or dojo *then* I could eat.

I would look in the mirror and feel physically revolted by how many imperfections I saw.

This was my rock bottom with my body. *This* was when I hated it the most.

If you would have told me that one day I would love eating again, that one day I'd find a healthy balance between nutritional eating and indulging—and that above all, my negative feelings around food would be totally healed—I would have never believed you.

But that's exactly what happened.

You can reach a point of total and complete self-loathing—and still heal.

I hope no one ever reaches such a low. I wish for that to be true from the bottom of my heart. But should you find yourself there, struggling to forgive yourself for whatever you are (the most bow-legged, buck-toothed, thin-lipped, browless, fattest person in the world) or struggling to forgive yourself for whatever you've done (slept around, hurt yourself, got addicted, hurt someone else, failed at a dream), you can still heal, completely.

Nothing is so bad that you can't forgive yourself.

And I do mean *nothing*.

Key Section Takeaways

- No matter what you've done to your body, you can learn to forgive yourself.
- No matter how much you hate or dislike your body, you can learn to love it.
- Your body, no matter how imperfect, is a blessing.
- Being grateful for that blessing will help you feel at peace with it.
- Cultivating honesty, trust, respect, and open communication with your body will improve your relationship with it.

- Healthy boundaries are essential to caring for your body, so that you and others know how to treat it well.

The Mind & Emotions Pillar

My father taught me to fear what I thought and felt. I can't tell you how many times he claimed, "You're crazy just like your mother. If you don't get your emotions under control, you're going to end up just like her."

The fact that I was usually upset when he said this seemed to serve as proof of the validity of his theory.

What I was overlooking at the time, however, was *why* I'd become upset in the first place.

If someone you love more than anything in the world (your father) tells you that you're the replica of the person they hate most in the world (your mother), it might be a natural response to burst into tears—at nine years old.

By my teen years, the tears had dried up and were replaced by anger. When it felt like my anger was more in control of my actions than I was, I worried even more that he was right about me. That my emotions were a problem. That my thoughts couldn't be trusted. That it was necessary to leash them or, better yet, lock them in a steel box and drop them in the ocean never to be seen again.

In a childhood like mine, children aren't allowed to take up emotional space. No one has the time or tolerance for feelings. Forget about emotional regulation.

Not a single adult in my life had mastered emotional regulation for themselves. How in the world could they teach me how to work with my difficult emotions when they were self-medicating their own traumas with alcohol and drugs? When they found it easier to assault someone than have a conversation with them?

My father was also abused as a child. His mother once hit him in the head with a skillet when she was drunk. He was also physically, emotionally, and mentally abused by his stepmother.

His father didn't protect him or any of his siblings when they were locked in closets for disobedience, left alone in the dark for hours.

There were also the struggles of poverty that plagued his family and the repercussions of how that hurts a kid growing up.

Anytime I had a birthday, or when we celebrated Christmas, my father liked to remind me that he'd grown up Jehovah's Witness.

"You're lucky because I didn't get presents growing up. We didn't celebrate birthdays."

It's not surprising to me that he became a heavy drinker, given his traumatic background, and the pressure of trying to change his fortune on his own. A childhood friend had once pointed out that the only difference between my mother's alcohol dependency and my father's was that he was better at hiding it. Later I'd hear the term "functional alcoholic."

While my father struggled with alcohol use, he also struggled with his anger. In the same breath he was telling me to take my feelings and lock them up in little boxes deep in my mind, he would scream, he would yell. He would throw things. He put his fist through the walls.

It would seem I came by my hotheadedness honestly.

The only difference was that I wasn't allowed to be angry. Whenever I pushed back against his abuse or toxicity, I was called selfish. "An ungrateful bitch, just like your mother."

Apparently, anger was only an emotion when I had it.

I also wasn't allowed to have thoughts. If I shared my perspective or a differing viewpoint, it was usually criticized. "You think you're so smart, don't you? I don't know how a smart person can be so stupid."

It was strange when my father had friends over and they would congratulate me on my good grades. They'd tell my father he should be so proud, and he would lean into this, bragging about how much I read, how much I loved books. He'd drop in self-effacing comments like, "Oh yes, I don't know where she gets it from. She's much smarter than me."

But behind closed doors it was a very different tune. He did appreciate my love of books. I will give him full credit for that. When I spent my allowance on books, he never complained.

However, if I tried to repeat anything I learned from those books, it became a battle. We had a screaming match about Napoleon Bonaparte once. I insisted that Napoleon died in exile as a traitor. My father would have bet everything he owned that Napoleon had died in Russia, as a war hero.

Sometimes the disagreements about the nature of reality were ridiculous, as with French generals. Most of the time they were not. When the fights were about my worth, about my right to have my own mind. My right to have feelings and especially my assertion that my reactions to his bad behavior were completely rational.

In case no one has told you, let me be the first: if someone treats you like a piece of shit, you are, *actually*, allowed to be insulted by this.

With my father, I fought to exist. But I was also a child. And a parent's true power over their child is love.

I adored him. Even now, after all that's happened, I still love him. One of the most heartbreaking aspects of healing my anger toward my father was to accept that beneath all the fury was still that deep well of love. It had not dried up. I'd only covered it over because it had been too painful to love him so much when he could not love me back.

To this day I have not forgotten what it felt like to be eight years old and convinced that my father had hung the moon.

But now my loyalty is to myself, and part of that loyalty demands that I do not allow others to mistreat me. Since he either cannot or will not restrain himself, he no longer has access to me.

This is disappointing, but not uncommon. Sometimes we can love someone very much and still need to keep them at a distance if that's what our well-being requires.

And my well-being requires it.

It may seem cruel to cut someone out of your life, but it is actually a kindness.

If that person was healthy, if they were at their best, they would never hurt you.

Healed people don't carelessly hurt others.

As a child I didn't understand that my father was also a damaged person who was only trying to hide his pain behind an iron mask. All I knew was that no matter how much I tried to hold on to those parts of myself, his constant assault eroded my self-belief. Having my thoughts and feelings consistently demeaned and dismissed as a child taught me to distrust my thoughts and feelings as an adult.

The mind can become a very messy place. If you're exposed to enough heartbreak and disappointment, all of your thoughts and feelings become a funhouse maze of mirrors. You will get lost in there. You'll think every reflection you see of yourself is truth, when it's not. It's pure distortion.

No matter how abandoned, how betrayed, how confused, how lost, or broken you are or have been, you can escape the funhouse.

My first step to escaping the funhouse was to stop fighting with myself.

In order to build honesty, trust, respect, and open communication with my thoughts and feelings, I had to first stop treating them like the enemy. Like problems to fix.

Think of honesty, trust, respect, and open communication as four strands of rope, braided together. Befriending our thoughts and emotions is like tying this rope around our waist so that no matter how the funhouse maze twists and turns, we can always find our way out.

One of the ways to move toward accepting our thoughts and feelings is to see the value in them.

It's in our best interests to accept our thoughts and feelings because they can give us a great deal of vital information, even when they're wrong or distorted. Vital information like how to navigate the maze, for starters. But accepting thoughts and feelings is not the same as acting upon them.

Nor is it the same as allowing them to control us.

When we befriend our thoughts and feelings, we can use them to our advantage rather than let them bring us down. Learning to listen to —but not be controlled by—my thoughts and feelings was a difficult task.

It was hard in the beginning because I had a lot of ideas about how my mind *should* be: stable, serene, brilliant, in perfect working order.

I know. Not only did I have these unrealistic expectations, but I also had a deep and pulsing fear that at any moment, I was going to self-implode like my mother was doing.

The process of befriending my emotions was the same as befriending the other parts of myself.

In the case of thoughts and feelings, I used honesty to cut through the self-deception. Whatever I was feeling was acceptable. No matter if I felt unhinged, furious, sad, depressed, lovesick, obsessed, addicted—okay. I could work with that. Even strong emotions like fear or suicidal ideations, I could work with those too. I might need professional help, but I could work with whatever was happening. What I would *not* do was lie to myself and tell myself I was *totally fine* and *absolutely great*, when I wasn't.

If you've ever began a sentence with "I know I shouldn't feel this way, but"—stop. You feel what you feel. Or perhaps, "I know I shouldn't think that but"—nope.

Your thoughts and feelings are what they are. When you reject them, you reject yourself.

You're resisting finding out who you really are.

If you've been suppressing or deprioritizing your thoughts and feelings for a long time like I was, it may take quite a bit of digging to figure out what it is you're actually feeling or thinking. I used therapy, meditation, and journaling to start reconnecting with this neglected pillar. But I encourage you to find whatever works for you.

I relied on cognitive behavioral therapy because I needed someone to guide me through the trauma review. I used stream-of-conscious freewriting because after I hit my page count, or the timer went off, I could reread what I wrote and have a better sense of what was going on in my head. I also implemented tonglen meditation because it teaches how to sit with and breathe through difficult emotions, how to work with the natural restless of the mind without being overcome by it.

And boy, is my mind restless.

I'm *really* good at thinking. I'm so good, in fact, that I made an entire career out of making up stories, called *fiction*.

My imagination is a wonderful gift. I am deeply grateful for it and so glad I have invested so much time and energy in its development. My creativity has allowed me to heal a lot—which I talk about in the next pillar's section.

I've also used my power of imagination to imagine a better life for myself. I've used it to pursue a passion that I love. And I use my imagination to solve the problems of my daily life.

But when I don't have control of my imagination, it can turn on me. When I don't give it something to do, like write stories, it will busy itself with imagining the worst possible scenario it can. It will have me jumping at shadows and preparing for catastrophes that will never strike.

This is why I'm pretty sure anxiety and imagination are twin sisters.

When anxiety is driving, my mind will have made ten contingency plans for each impending disaster, and all before breakfast.

What if I start losing my vision and have to get shots in my eyeballs? What will I do if my wife dies in a horrible car accident? What if I'm diagnosed with cancer? What if we lose our jobs and can't get new ones? What if I lose all my money in a Ponzi scheme? What if a zombie apocalypse breaks out? What if I spontaneously became pregnant? Would my lesbian marriage survive it?

This is the nonsense I'm dealing with here.

But we can befriend the nonsense. We can develop a certain level of detachment so that we see the thoughts with a bit of distance. We feel the feelings but don't lose ourselves in them.

Once you become friendly toward your thoughts and feelings rather than critical of them, they will be infinitely more manageable.

When we strike this balance, we have all the power of our heart and mind at our disposal, without losing ourselves to its current.

Those ten-eyed, green-skinned, yellowed-nailed monsters known as your thoughts and feelings just wanted to be loved after all.

This balance and detachment can be achieved by building self-awareness. And there are many ways we can build self-awareness. My favorites are meditation, mindfulness practices, therapy, journaling, shadow work, and self-reflection.

These are the techniques that have taught me that thoughts and feelings are not a problem.

They only become a problem when we are too scared to look at them and they are allowed to control our behavior because of the power we've given them.

In my case, I didn't want to look because I was afraid my father was right about me. When I finally drummed up the courage to look, and then even more courage to figure out what I was seeing, I was set free.

So look.

Be brave enough to look. Then be brave enough to love what you find.

Even the darkness.

This will change everything.

Key Section Takeaways

- It is important to trust our thoughts and feelings.
- A healthy relationship with this pillar isn't about getting our thoughts and feelings sorted out or making them better. It's about striking a healthy balance between seeing our thoughts and feelings clearly and honoring the wisdom they provide, while not letting the thoughts and feelings control our behavior.
- We can learn to befriend our thoughts and feelings through healthy coping mechanisms like meditation, therapy, and journaling.
- Cultivating honesty, trust, respect, and open communication with our thoughts and feelings will help us identify mental and emotional strengths, like imagination. Only then can we use these abilities to make our lives better.

The Spirit Pillar

Your spirit pillar represents your relationship with meaning, purpose, creativity, and joy.

For me, connecting with my creativity and using it to heal myself and others gives my life meaning and purpose. It's also a source of joy.

It's no exaggeration when I say that my creativity saved my life. Creativity is a powerful tool of self-expression and problem-solving, and can be used to find meaning in our experiences, especially the terrible ones.

Creativity has the unique ability to take something awful and turn it into something beautiful. Creativity can make sense of the horrifying experiences that we've endured and transmute it into something powerful and worthy of being shared.

I often hear, "But Kory, I can't do what you do. I'm not a creative person."

Wrong.

Everyone is creative. Everyone has an imagination.

It is a myth that only some people are creative and imaginative.

Often we look at exceptionally good art, stories, movies, music, and we decide, ah, that person is really creative. They're so talented. They have a *gift*. There's no way *I* could do that. I'm just not an imaginative person.

But creativity is not a skill. When I was painting on a little easel at five years old, I had no skill in painting. When I was writing—heaven help me—emo poetry in my diary at sixteen, I had no skill in writing poetry. That would come later while earning an MFA in poetry.

We often confuse someone's *skills* with innate ability.

Everyone is creative. Not everyone has the same creative *skills*.

I write well because I have studied it, written millions of words, published over thirty books, and use the skill almost every day.

Contrarily, I play piano very poorly. I've only ever taken a handful of lessons, in childhood, *long ago*, culminating in a nerve-wracking recital in which I played "When The Saints Go Marching In." As an adult, I know how to play two random songs, neither of which are about saints.

Does my inability to play the piano well mean I'm not a creative person?

Of course not.

All humans are capable of creative work.

Imagination is also a creative skill.

You can develop your imagination *skill* by reading more fiction and indulging in daydreaming and planning. By designing and building things. By problem-solving. By playing the "What if..." game.

What if I woke up with a tail tomorrow?

What if I had the power to transform into a plant at will?

What if I had a free year of all-expenses-paid travel—where would I go?

What if I walked into the office and told my narcissistic boss to shove her stapler right up her—?

What would happen if I ran into my ex and they were holding hands with the hottest person alive? What would I do?

If you can think through any of these scenarios, then you have an imagination.

It's just that you may also have a tendency to look at someone like me and think you don't have one because, again, you're confusing skill with innate ability.

I started developing my imagination skill *very* early in childhood as a way to escape my difficult circumstances. When I could imagine better, or hell, just imagine myself anywhere else, it helped me to cope with what was going on at home. I can remember playing imagination games and loving books and stories—all of which require imagination—when I was as young as two or three. Maybe even younger.

That means when it comes to my imagination, I have about *forty years* of skill development under my belt. So it's not fair for someone to look at me and say they have no imagination just because they haven't been honing the skill for forty years.

You can develop creative *skills* like painting, musical ability, and writing with practice. Don't look at the hours someone has put into a project or skill and declare yourself unimaginative and uncreative just because you haven't invested the same amount of time they have.

As a writer I may never be on the same level as James Baldwin or Mary Oliver, but that doesn't mean I should give up. It doesn't mean I'm incapable of incredible things. Hell, one day I might surprise myself.

You might also be blocked from developing your creativity or imagination because you devalue it.

Many of us were told, "Grow up. Get real. Get your head out of the clouds. Come back to reality." Rhetoric like this makes us reject our innate creativity and imagination rather than develop it.

But no matter how society, family, or shitty teachers may try, they cannot scold your creativity away. They may convince you that you don't have it, but you do.

It's only a matter of developing that innate creativity into viable skills.

So congrats. You're a creative.

And if you'd love to explore ways to develop and unleash your creativity, I highly recommend Julia Cameron's *The Artist's Way* series, for connecting with that part of you. I have gone back to those books for inspiration and direction many times over the years.

Creativity isn't limited to the arts either. Sure, musicians, artists, writers, and actors are some of the most easily recognizable creatives, but we also find creative work in business, science, education, construction, manufacturing, and countless other fields. When a teacher is working hard to figure out twenty-five different ways to teach a lesson so that all of his students understand it, that requires a lot of creativity.

I also currently work with an environmental NGO, Community Conservation. Most of the people involved have a scientific background, but we still have an endless need for creativity when it comes to solving the constant funding problems that plague any nonprofit. Or when we have to come up with sustainable, community-based solutions to complicated environmental problems.

Creativity is, by definition, problem-solving. And it is limitless in its potential. That means it can be used anywhere, at any time.

And I highly encourage you to use your imagination and creativity to improve the quality of your life and the condition of your mind. Put them to good use in service of your well-being.

Creativity is a powerful healing tool in your human toolbox. It'd be a shame not to use this great tool you already have.

You do not have to be skilled to reap the benefits of creativity either.

Use it all the same.

Just note that when we are talking about using creativity to heal ourselves, we're not talking about accomplishment. I've made the mistake of confusing the two myself, and it burned me out.

The creative work you produce doesn't have to be profitable, approved of by others, or even liked in order to be valuable.

If you do decide to add more creativity to your days—and I really hope you do—please note that having people criticize your creativity is a quick way to disconnect you from it. In fact, it might have been criticism that made you incorrectly believe you're not creative to begin with. We must be sure to protect ourselves from anything that will trigger this self-rejection of our creativity.

For that reason, I'd have some boundaries around who you show your work to.

Not everyone can be trusted to be kind or even helpful in their feedback.

It's true that if you stick with a particular outlet for creativity—writing, painting, music, woodworking, welding, whatever—you might get very good at that skill over time. And as a by-product of that skillfulness you might receive approval, be liked, or turn a profit. But then that skill has become a job. And when a creative skill becomes a job, it no longer has the same healing effects as it had before because expectations, deadlines, and criticism have come into the mix.

A creative job can connect to meaning and purpose. Mine certainly does. But I suffer when I don't also have a creative outlet that I do only for me, for the sole purpose of my joy and happiness.

I could probably write a whole book on how to keep joy and meaning alive if you do creative work, but that's not what this book is about.

This book is about building a healthy relationship with yourself. And when it comes to building our relationship with our third pillar—our spirit—I just want to be clear that it isn't about being *good* at something. Skill has nothing to do with your well-being, unless of course we count the confidence boost we get from doing something well.

Having a relationship with this pillar is about figuring out what lights you up. About learning to prioritize your joy and play.

Every time we indulge in creativity, joy, play, happiness, curiosity, we're telling ourselves that what we want *matters*. That our freedom *matters*. That we are allowed to use our life however we want.

It's a radical act, to be joyful in a world even as it falls apart.

Easier said than done, I know.

We aren't really allowed to play as adults. We aren't allowed to have an ounce of joy in a world that takes itself way too seriously. It might be especially hard for you to connect with your spirit if you were forced to grow up quickly. If you were moving from one crisis to the next all your life, when were you able to develop the space and freedom to connect with your creativity, playfulness, and joy?

As a kid, I spent a lot of energy trying to protect my mom. When I was with my father and he caught me playing or daydreaming or expressing joy in his presence, he would put me to work.

That's why my embrace of a creative life only happened because I was trying to make a living off it. I convinced myself it wasn't play when it was *business*. When it was a tool to make money and meet my financial needs. Only then was it okay to do something I also happened to love doing.

Fortunately, very slowly I grew—and I'm still growing—out of this.

In case no one has told you, I want you to know it's okay to "waste" time being joyful. It's not a waste at all. The joy you store up in your heart will keep you alive.

Don't let anyone—not even yourself—tell you that you don't have time for your own happiness.

Wear your joy like a shield against that bullshit.

And know that when you're suffering, when you're grieving, one of the most powerful and transformative moves you can make is to pick up the pen, or paintbrush, or start dancing, or singing your heart out.

Do something, anything, with all that pain inside you.

Creativity will help you to shape it, shift it, use it, and release it.

You can use creativity to get it all out.

That's what I do.

And what my mother had tried to do.

She'd been an amazing singer.

It's actually how my parents met.

When she was eighteen, she traveled around the country visiting different churches with my grandmother. My grandmother was a traveling pastor at the time. Nana gave guest sermons and my mother sang.

It was my father's mother who told him, "You have to come to church and meet the pastor's daughter. She has the voice of an angel."

He rolled up to the church the next Sunday on his rumbling motorcycle and liked what he saw. Only by then his brother had made his move, gifting my mother with a Bible and trying to sell her on the possibility of their bright future together.

Instead, my mother rode off into the sunset on the back of my father's motorcycle. Three months later, they were married. I know this because the dates were written in the Bible she later gifted to me, a sort of interesting family record of the summer she'd turned nineteen.

I remember my mother singing a lot when I was little, and I don't know what angels sound like, but she did have a powerful voice. A rich contralto voice, and she loved to sing Melissa Etheridge, Tracy Chapman, and Whitney Houston songs.

And I loved to listen to her.

The woman who sat on our kitchen counter with a beer balanced on her lap, singing her heart out to Tracy Chapman's "Give Me One Reason," seemed like a very different woman than the one I'd find sobbing alone in the bathroom when she thought no one could hear her.

Singing was the only *healthy* way my mother used to transmute her pain, to be heard, and when she gave up singing, she suffered greatly because of it.

She no longer had anywhere to direct all that heartache.

In prison, my father turned to art. He drew dozens of Disney characters and sent them to me in the mail. I was always so excited to get his latest batch of work, thrilled in the unbridled way only a six-year-old can manage. When I asked why he stopped drawing, he said it'd helped him cope with being in prison. Now that he was out, he didn't need it anymore.

I can't help but wonder how much happier he might have been if he'd continued to explore his interest in art.

Similarly, when I'm writing or doing creative work, I am also my most steady, my most stable, mentally and emotionally. True, my body suffers if I sit too much—gotta love that chronic lower back pain—but that can be managed.

When I go too long between projects or let life get in the way, my mental health begins to suffer. All that restless and wild energy gets snappish. It starts to twist back on me, ready to bite the hand that feeds. Remember what I said about anxiety and imagination being twins? Guess who comes to dinner when I haven't channeled that energy through creative outlets in a while?

It's vital to my mental health that I use my creativity regularly.

There are three ways that I use creativity in service of my well-being:

1. To find meaning and purpose in experiences.
2. As a form of self-expression.
3. As a tool for problem-solving.

Writing *Who Killed My Mother?* certainly helped me to make sense of my family history, our shared trauma, and to contextualize the experiences I'd had with my mother. In doing so, I healed my relationship with her. Emotionally I went from "Why wasn't I enough? Why couldn't you shape up and be a good mom to me?" to "Of course she was like that. After everything that happened to her, there's no way she could have been any different. The neglect was never personal."

Coming to understand her for who she was and why she'd done what she'd done allowed me to remove all the bad blood between us and keep only love, forgiveness, and some bittersweet grief.

That's the power of creativity.

I also use creativity to express myself in my fiction. What to do with all my big emotions, all my negative experiences, and a desperate longing to connect with others?

Write stories, of course!

In *Shadows in the Water*, I created Louie Thorne, the embodiment of all my darkness, restlessness, and anger.

In the *City* series, Grace learns how to move through grief and redefine her reason for living.

In *Jack and the Fire Eater*, Jack has to take a good long look at the abuse he endured from his father and how to overcome it.

Sure, these are murder mysteries and thrillers and fantasies meant to delight and entertain. But they were also not-so-subtle attempts to try and understand myself, my beliefs, and the events of my life. My characters' experiences were my experiences. If not literally, certainly emotionally.

True, my life hasn't been full of *actual* demons, but my family came close enough. And you can draw a line from the emotional landscape of my characters, from their fears and hopes, straight to turmoil of my own.

Writing those stories allowed me to share those experiences with others who could read them, delight (or not) in them, and react to them without ever knowing just how close those tales cut to my own heart.

That's why my memoir was such a departure for me. When I write fiction, I put on a mask. I try to seduce readers with my little fiction dance, hoping you'll never know how much of the performance was really me or just make-believe.

When I wrote *Who Killed My Mother?*, there was no mask. I had to muster up a lot of courage to share it.

You don't have to go as far with your creativity as I have. You get to decide how much of yourself you'd like to reveal and share with others.

Your creativity, above all, is meant to be in service to *you*.

Use it to express what you think and feel. Use it to get to know yourself. Use it to understand yourself and your experiences better. Use it as a form of play, figuring out what you really love. Use it to discover joy and connection.

Creativity can also teach you a lot of things.

How to solve your problems.

How to practice hope.

You don't know a project or idea will work out when you start it. You only hope it will. In the same vein, creativity teaches you flexibility.

You might have a grand vision about how something can be created, only to discover that once you start making it, the project goes in an entirely different direction. When this happens we have to bend and move with our creation if we want to see it through to completion.

Creativity also teaches you open-mindedness. It teaches you to consider the possibilities. You need to explore ideas and possible solutions when you're trying to make something. Your mind gets quite the workout, and that's a good thing. Remember what I said happens when we don't give it something to do?

All of these skills—hope, flexibility, problem-solving, expression, joy, and open-mindedness—will serve you well in life, not just in your creative endeavors.

My relationship with creativity is certainly the largest and most developed aspect of my relationship with my spirit pillar. Creativity allows me to be honest with myself about what matters to me, what lights me up, what gives me joy. It helps me build trust every time I take on a new and often intimidating project. It fosters respect for play and joy and curiosity. It teaches me to listen to myself and what I want and need despite the overbearing expectations of others.

But creativity is just one expression of this pillar.

Apart from your creativity, there are other areas of your life where you can connect to your spirit.

In your work, whatever work it is that you do, are you connected to a sense of purpose? Do you feel that the work you do matters? It doesn't have to be easy work, but it is best if it's meaningful work.

Can you fill in this blank: My work matters to me because_____

Do you like the answer, assuming you have an answer at all?

If not, are you in the wrong occupation? Or do you need to start thinking about your work in a new way? Sometimes the biggest change that's needed is a mindset shift.

If I asked you what your ten favorite ways to play are, could you make that list quickly and easily? What about if I asked what are the ten things that bring you the most joy?

And how often do you indulge in these joyful and playful things? Often?

Or are you too busy adulting?

If you are a spiritual or religious person, you can also use those beliefs to find meaning. To paint your life and experiences with the brush of purpose. Your beliefs—assuming they are not used to hurt yourself or other people—can be used to help you to be more honest, trusting, respectful, and to connect with something greater than yourself.

Not sure which area of your life would most benefit from a sense of meaning and purpose? Then ask yourself in what areas of your life could you stand to grow.

Everything I've mentioned in this pillar—curiosity, play, joy, meaning, purpose, creativity, imagination—all points to growth.

Where and how do you want to grow?

Because to live is to grow.

Unlike an acorn that must sprout wherever the squirrel buried it, no matter if that bit of land is then covered by a slab of concrete, our roots are mobile.

We can shimmy out of the muck whenever we want and scuttle off to more favorable pastures with a bit of effort.

Let's not waste our power to do so.

Key Section Takeaways

- Everyone is creative.
- Creativity is not the same as skill, though you may develop creative skills like painting, musical ability, writing, or using your imagination if you practice them enough.
- The results of your creativity don't have to be "good" in order to be beneficial. You will gain countless benefits from using creativity even if you don't produce something "good."

- Cultivating a sense of purpose can ground us and provide a deep sense of well-being and peace in life.
- Meaning and purpose can also be nurtured in our work or occupation, as well as through a connection to a higher power.

The Connection Pillar

Full disclosure: this is the pillar I struggled with the most. You might think that surely it was the mind, that place was a real dump when I started renovating it. Or maybe the body pillar was the worst since it had endured so much mistreatment.

Wrong.

My connection pillar really was worse than all the rest. Not only because it was, for lack of a better metaphor, practically ground to dust by the time I started to take a good look at it. But also because I had *no* desire to repair it.

At least with my body, mind & emotions, and spirit, I'd *wanted* to get better. I'd wanted to heal and could see the value in improving those areas of my well-being.

When it came to connection, I had been so disappointed by people over the course of my life, in every capacity imaginable—parents, family, friendships, romantic connections, you name it—that the idea of trusting other people, putting myself out there, being vulnerable, being judged and assessed as worthy of love and affection—*no*.

Absolutely not.

It was unfathomable.

It felt like losing people I loved and depended on had been a lifelong experience. I was not interested in signing up for more of that.

The first time I lost someone it happened as a double whammy.

When I was four years old, officers burst into the little house I was sharing with my parents. My father was pushed to the floor of the living room and handcuffed.

I was too young to understand what was happening. One of the officers was also trying to distract me, keep me from watching the scene unfold, but I remember enough.

My mother crying, her hands over her mouth, my father's wide eyes of surprise as his hands were bound behind his back.

I'd been pulled into the kitchen adjacent to the living room. An officer was sitting on one of the kitchen chairs, trying to block my view of the living room, where my parents and the other officers were.

"Tell me about your book," he'd said. He'd pointed at the book in my hand. It was my favorite book about sea creatures. At the time, I would tell everyone who would listen about how I was going to be a marine biologist when I grew up.

But I didn't want to tell the officer about the book, I wanted to see what was going on. I was trying to understand what was happening, why the officers had pushed my father to the floor, why they'd cuffed his hands behind his back, why they were dragging him from the house while my mother watched in silent horror.

Shortly after this, I also lost my best friend.

My best friend was a black Lab named Buddy that I'd had all my life. When my father was incarcerated, my mother decided to move us from North Carolina, where we'd been living with my father, back to Nashville, where she was from.

But it would just be the two of us returning to Nashville. Buddy wasn't allowed to come.

I watched as they loaded him into a cage in the back of the animal control truck. As the truck pulled away, I ran screaming into the street after him. My mother and grandmother caught me, held me back. I only struggled harder.

Buddy was barking like mad, jerking from side to side in his metal cage in the back of the truck, obviously upset by the confusion of the situation and me screaming his name as only a hysterical four-year-old could.

Watching him be driven away from me tore my heart in two.

I could still visit my father in prison, but Buddy was gone forever.

From there, the losses only compounded. My mother, who I remembered as being stable during those early years, slowly lost her mind when we moved back to Nashville. Her love for me was always evident. She never spoke to me the way my father did. But her behavior became increasingly erratic and belligerent with others. I was often put in dangerous or neglectful situations.

Getting my needs met as a child felt like an impossible choice.

With my mother, I could be loved. She was very good at making me feel loved, making me feel seen and heard. She validated my experiences sincerely and often. Even as an adult, when I would express fear or doubt about my career or achieving my dreams, she was quick to say, "Of course you can do this. Look how much you've overcome! Look at what an amazing person you are. You can do this, baby. If anyone can do this, it's *you*."

With her I always felt free to be whoever I was and still loved for it.

But my mother wasn't good at keeping me safe. There was no structure, no stability in my life, when I stayed with her. Things could be good one minute and dissolve into chaos the next. She could be happy and laughing, making some of the funniest jokes you've ever heard in your life, and then be sobbing her heart out and threatening to kill herself in front of me.

With my father it was the opposite.

Constantly, I was told how I was lacking, how I failed to measure up, how I was worthless, a lost cause, a replica of my insane mother. When I tried to defend myself or speak up for myself, I was met with punishments, derision, condescension, insults, or rage. I walked on eggshells trying not to trigger his anger, his abuse, or provoke him by simply daring to breathe in the same space.

I never felt loved by him, but he did provide structure.

He was a *very* structured man, to the point of controlling.

Yet I never got a call in the night saying he'd gone missing and his car had been found in a ditch seventy miles from where it should have been. He never failed to pick me up from school. He was consistent in a way that my mother could have never achieved.

He never forgot to buy groceries or feed me. He always signed school forms on time.

If I needed something like clothes, shoes, a backpack, he would provide it. He might complain. "I need a... I need a... I need a... I should've named you Anita, all the shit you ask for."

But he did get me what I asked for.

The cool Adidas jacket everyone was wearing in eighth grade.

Cars on two separate occasions. A credit card for emergencies. He even sent me on a school trip to Europe. Anyone looking in would have said, "Kory is a lucky girl. Her dad sure does love her."

No matter how generous, the thrill of these extravagant gifts never lasted. These momentary displays of adoration rang hollow.

And my father was quick to remind me how blessed and lucky I was whenever he criticized me to tears. After he beat me so hard with the buckle end of a belt that I was black and blue for three weeks. When he cut me down until I felt like the smallest, most worthless creature in the world.

You have no idea how good you've got it. You have no idea what pain is.

My father was a good provider, but he could not love me.

My mother loved me, but she could not provide.

This polarization between the two of them instilled in me the erroneous belief that connection required such impossible choices. To receive love, something must always be sacrificed. That I could have my needs met, be spoiled even, if I also turned a blind eye to cruelty, abuse, and misuse. I could be loved and cherished, but only at the expense of stability and safety.

This message was only further complicated and compounded when I was outed in ninth grade.

At fourteen, I developed my first crush on a girl. I'd met her at a school dance, then saw her again weeks later at the county fair.

The county fair was a big deal in the small town where I grew up. It came once a year, filling the fairgrounds with its creaky carnival rides and game booths. The scent of fried corndogs, pickles, and funnel cakes greased the air.

Not long after I'd arrived at the fair, I spotted my crush. Pretty quickly we ditched our respective friends in order to hang out with each other. I was as excited as any lovesick fourteen-year-old girl was. I got up the nerve to talk to her, to ride some rickety carnival rides with her. We even skipped school the next day and hung out a little bit before my mom took her home.

I'd thought it was the best twenty-four hours of my life until it blew up in my face when I went back to school. When I walked through the doors the following day, something had changed.

First of all, everyone was looking at me.

People were whispering and laughing. I went up to my best friend's locker to ask her what was going on and she slammed it shut in my face and stormed away. I tried several more times to talk to her, but she wouldn't even speak to me.

The name-calling came next: *dyke, whore, queer*.

I knew what these words meant since my father had called my mother such names.

Then the whispering, giggling, and pointing escalated to pushing.

The one place I'd always been safe, that I could count on—school—turned into just another battleground.

I went from being relatively liked to a pariah overnight.

This bullying only complicated the treacherous dance I was already trying to navigate: how could I be true to who I was, how could I want what I wanted, need what I needed, and still be loved for it?

It felt like I couldn't be. That here was just another impossible choice.

My mother was the one who had outed me to my father, giving him all the "proof" he needed that there was something inherently wrong with me.

He had come down to pick me up for the holidays. He kept pestering my mother with questions like, "What if she's having sex? What if she gets pregnant?"

Finally, my mother, who'd kept my confidences for about two years at this point, finally exclaimed, "For fuck's sake, David, she's sleeping with *girls*. She won't get pregnant."

When my father asked me if I was gay, I said yes, though I wasn't actually sure at the time.

He cried, and his tears made me feel like the shittiest daughter who'd ever lived.

Since it was a six-hour car ride back to his place, it also made for a very awkward trip.

Quickly my sexual orientation became just another weapon in his arsenal. He would trot it out whenever he wanted to convince me he was right.

"What do you know? You're so confused that you think you're gay just because your whore of a mother sleeps with everything that moves."

It's no wonder that my romantic relationships in my teens and early twenties were disastrous. I gave people a lot of passes for mistreating me. Remember the cute girl from my first high school dance? About two years after that dance, I would let her convince me to crawl into the trunk of her car and be driven across town to her house. *Then* I hid in that trunk until her mom left for her third-shift job so I could sneak into the house and we could spend the night together without being seen. That was the plan, anyway.

Until she fell asleep and forgot me in the trunk of the car all night. Lucky for me, Toyota Corolla trunks open from the inside.

This is the kind of bad behavior I'd come to expect from others—lying, cheating, manipulation, disregard, and betrayal—because I'd come to believe that to connect with someone meant I was agreeing to be hurt by them. That in exchange for love or affection, I would always have to leave some part of myself at the door.

But true love and connection should not be an impossible choice.

It can't be this *or* that.

You can learn to form relationships that keep your well-being in the picture, that account for your emotional needs and your physical needs at the same time.

You can learn to do this even if, right now, you're so desperate you'd let someone put you in the trunk of their car if it meant you felt wanted, even for an hour.

Even if you're silly enough to see the pillow they put in that trunk for you and think, *Oh how sweet* instead of *What the actual fu—*

The thing about a strong connection pillar is not about learning to have complete faith in others again. I still take most people on a case-by-case basis. I probably always will.

It's about learning to trust yourself so completely that *you* know you will be okay even if the worst happens.

Even if the parents who were supposed to love you abuse you.

Even if your best friend in the world stops talking to you without explaining why.

Even if the whole school outcasts you.

Even if your first love forgets you in a trunk when you're sixteen, and when you break up for the final time at twenty, it's only because she's cheating on you with a stripper who she moves into your shared duplex without even asking you first—

Yes, you will survive it all.

I'm not saying it won't hurt. I'm only saying it won't break you.

And it's not about you getting perfect enough to be lovable either.

Having a healthy relationship with connection means that no matter what happens, you know you deserve love, respect, and fair treatment just as you are.

You are worthy *now*.

If you're reading this, however, and thinking, *I don't know. This connection business still seems too risky to me.*

Then let me tell you about the alternatives.

One alternative is to lock up your heart and make the world as small and controllable as you can. That's what my father did. He prided himself on becoming the monster after all those years of suffering at the hands of his abusers. He always strove to make sure he was the baddest guy in the room.

My mother had the opposite approach. She invited all the monsters inside and said, "Do your worst." And then they certainly tried.

But there is a middle ground between these two extremes. You can keep your heart open. You can be a loving person, and also have a password—or an armed ballistic missile system—at the ready to keep out whatever needs to be kept out.

This ballistic missile system is called boundaries, by the way.

Establishing boundaries in our relationships is a critical component of open communication in relationships. But in order to establish boundaries, we need to have an awareness of what we need and want from our relationships.

How else will we know what to draw the boundary line around?

I got clear on my needs and wants (and a lot of dislikes as well) during my years-long vow of celibacy. When I stopped looking after everyone else's needs long enough to figure out what I needed.

This is where honesty comes in. We have to be honest with ourselves about what we need to be happy and healthy.

For a long time, I gave my family excuses. It's okay that Mom is so erratic because it's clear that she loves me. It's okay that Dad speaks to me the way he does because he had a rough childhood too and he works hard to pay the bills on time. It's okay to settle for less because this is the best I can get.

No.

That's not being honest with yourself. Getting honest with myself meant I had to realize that I needed more.

I needed people in my life who were kind and affirming and validating. And I wanted people who were trustworthy and consistent. I wanted someone I could rely on.

Someone who wouldn't tear me down or try to punish me for things that weren't my fault. Someone who trusted my thoughts and feelings and wasn't always trying to gaslight me or blame me for their bad behavior.

First I would become that for myself, which was harder to do than I thought it would be.

Only then did I slowly let people into my circle who demonstrated these traits as well.

Being honest also meant acknowledging that I wasn't yet the kind of person who could be there for others in these ways. In the beginning, I was not my best self. I had a lot of work to do in the relationship department—in friendships and romantic partnerships—because my previous connections taught me some really bad habits when it came to loving and connecting with others.

I was going to have to unlearn those habits and replace them with better skills if I was to be the kind of friend I wanted people to be for me, the kind of partner I wanted for myself.

Trust is about keeping the heart open. It can be scary to give people a chance. To see if they can add value to your life rather than detract from it. You might assume that trust in the connection pillar is about learning to trust other people. And yes, learning to trust other people is a wonderful skill to have.

But trust in the connection pillar is actually more about learning to trust *yourself* with other people. Learning to trust that you won't throw your own needs and wants out the window the second someone asks you to. Or more brazenly, *expects* you to.

Trust is also about believing with your whole heart that it is okay to put yourself out there and find your person or your tribe, because you believe you have more to gain than to lose. And you no longer believe yourself to be this delicate flower who will blow away in the wind if someone steps on you.

You know you're strong enough to handle a bit of bad behavior if it helps you to weed out who should and who shouldn't be invited to the next round of interviews. Believing in your strength and believing that the right people will come along is a big part of trust when it comes to connections.

With respect, I had to learn to respect the needs I had in my connections. Respect what my feelings and instincts were telling me about people. When a behavior or situation didn't feel okay, I stopped pretending it was okay. I had to love myself enough not to settle for less.

I also stopped saying yes to things I didn't want to say yes to, just because someone asked. This taught me to respect my time, my attention, and my energy as important.

Our fourth attribute of open communication is very important in this pillar.

Communication is always a two-way street. In this context, it's important that we learn to listen to ourselves, and then we can communicate those needs and boundaries to others. We also need to hear what other people are trying to say about their needs and learn to respect their boundaries.

Sometimes people don't react well to our boundaries. That feels awful. But we can develop a tolerance for this level of unpleasantness by reminding ourselves that it is so much better than the alternative: how awful we feel when we play the role of doormat.

The payoff of open communication is to be truly seen and heard by other humans.

Often we don't even want to be seen. The communication itself is tricky. We often don't say what we mean. Or if we do, someone claims we're too blunt. Or we had a "tone," or we didn't make enough eye contact. Or the eye contact was too aggressive.

The pitfalls are endless.

But the payoff for doing this work was far more incredible than I could've ever imagined.

Ten out of ten. Highly recommend.

Key Chapter Takeaways

- There are four pillars to your well-being: the body pillar, the mind & emotions pillar, the spirit pillar, and the connections pillar.
- Investing equally in these four areas will build a strong and stable relationship with yourself.
- The stronger your relationship with yourself, the more you will experience peace, confidence, self-compassion, strength, resilience, and self-love—all of which are natural by-products of your relationship with yourself.
- The way to develop a relationship with yourself is by applying the four key attributes of honesty, trust, respect, and open communication to each of the four pillars.
- Our ability to make healthy connections with others requires us to keep our needs in the picture.
- Keeping one's heart open despite heartbreak and disappointment requires courage, self-belief, and commitment. But it is better to live bravely with an open heart than to live half a life with a closed one.

SELF-CARE: WHAT IT IS AND WHAT IT ISN'T

Despite the recent obsession with the practice of self-care, the Oxford Dictionary [6] tells us that the term *self-care* has been used since as early as 1567, and is defined as "the activity of taking care of one's own health, appearance, or well-being."

When we hear the word *self-care* these days, it seems as though self-care is really only a matter of buying yourself the right thing.

Bath bombs, skincare, beauty products, a healthy diet plan, an exercise program, a vacation to Bali.

Many businesses make a profit by preying on our insecurities and convincing us to buy a product to fix our woes.

Or they sell us a product with the promise of fast results, knowing that dopamine hit of satisfaction will have us running back to buy more. What they don't tell us is that in both cases, easy come, easy go.

It's often no time at all before we find ourselves back at square one, wondering why nothing works, why we're still tired, why we're still stressed, why we're still lost and confused and overwhelmed.

I can't tell you how many times I've told someone, "I don't feel well," only to be told, "You just need to eat better, sleep more, get some exercise, some fresh air and sunshine."

This is all great advice, but the issue is that all of it falls under the body pillar.

And as I've already outlined, one standing pillar does not a temple make. We invest all this time and energy into building one pillar and wonder why we can't find any relief.

So how do we practice self-care in a way that will amount to something?

What does self-care look like in the context of honesty, trust, respect, and open communication?

If our well-being is a relationship that we build with ourselves, then self-care tasks are the practices we do in order to *build* that relationship.

The stronger and healthier that relationship, the stronger and healthier your well-being will be and the more capable you will be in the face of difficulty and challenge.

We call this imperviousness to difficulty resilience. The more likely a person is to overcome and survive a hardship, the more resilient they are. I have a whole chapter about it later in this book.

But what I'd like to say for now is that resiliency can make a bomb blast feel like a mosquito bite.

Resiliency allows us to bounce back from loss much quicker. Resiliency improves the quality of our lives.

This is another reason why it's so important to keep viewing our wellness as a relationship, because relationships go through cycles. They get tested and they get stressed. Sometimes a relationship needs a lot of loving attention. Other times it's easy breezy lemon squeezy.

The more resilient your relationships, the more likely they are to survive these tests.

It's the same for your relationship with yourself. The more resilient it is, the easier it will be for you to navigate this minefield called life.

Think of self-care tasks as deposits into your resiliency bank. You want a nice fat bank balance. Most of the time you'll be wondering if it's adding up to anything. Then one day, a horrible, unexpected bill will come, and you'll suddenly be incredibly grateful that you have all these healthy coping mechanisms and loving relationships and good habits. They will in fact be the reason you pull through this dicey situation when compared to someone else who got hit with the same shocking bill when their account was in the negative.

Do not think just because you are a resilient person, you can't overdraw on your resiliency account.

I have had a negative account myself more than once. We call this burnout. Don't live like this if you can help it.

Making sure we are practicing enough self-care is one way to ensure we don't burn out. But while hot baths, massages, and a good book are lovely ways to relax—and relaxing is important—these actions will not necessarily help us build a good relationship with ourselves or increase our resiliency.

We must invest widely, across all four pillars, if we want the benefits of resiliency.

Those old, dilapidated temples are still standing because they are very resilient and what helps them to remain standing is because the weight of that heavy roof is dispersed across multiple pillars.

However, many of us invest all of our—very limited—time into self-care tasks that fall under the body pillar only, like eating well, sleeping, exercising, but still feel like something is lacking even if we work really hard on this area of our life.

Then we get cheated on, or a pet we love dies, or we lose our job and it's pizza every night for a week and the only exercise we're getting are all those thumb-flex reps with the remote or internet-scrolling on our phone.

Now the resiliency bank balance is tipping into the red again.

A more even distribution of weight across the pillars will be more protective than an intense concentration in one area.

Let's imagine you got sick. God forbid, but let's pretend for a moment.

You get sick and that's a direct hit to your body pillar. If you've been actively investing in the other three pillars and your resiliency bank account is looking nice and developed, then you will move through your illness with advantages.

With a strong connections pillar, you'll have a community to draw strength and support from. In the practical sense, someone makes soup or a casserole so you don't have to cook. Or they come over to walk the dog.

With a strong spirit pillar, you could use your creativity to process the experience of being ill. You will be more likely to connect with a sense of gratitude for all the help you're receiving at that time, from friends, family, doctors, or a sense of divine intervention. Maybe you can still find joy in a day despite your illness. Many famous creatives have spent whole parts of their lives bedridden. Frida Kahlo, Flannery O'Connor, Stephen Hawking, to name a few.

We don't have to let our mobility issues or poor health rob us of our joy—or so I tell myself when my back pain has me in tears.

With a strong mind & emotions pillar, you'll have coping skills at your disposal to sit with and process the emotional challenge of being sick. You'll have a better capacity to work with fear, and doubt and uncertainty. You'll know how to work with and through negative thought spirals or anxiety.

All of these examples are to illustrate that you can draw strength from other pillars—other aspects of your relationship with yourself—when one or two areas take a hit. That's resiliency.

When people say, "I tried self-care and it didn't work. I still feel the same," it's often because the self-care is not equally distributed across all the pillars. The efforts were focused on immediate short-term relief rather than long-term resiliency.

This is understandable. When we are in pain, and especially if that pain is nearly unbearable, we want relief however we can get it. The quicker the better.

But the best self-care will have a long-term view.

That is why it is better to do even one small task in each area than invest all your energy into one pillar hoping it will dramatically change your life.

The exception to this is if you already have two or three strong pillars and there are only one or two areas left in your life to improve. Let's say you have a great relationship with your body and with connection, for example, but your mind & emotions are a mess. Also, you don't feel so confident in your relationship with your spirit.

In that case, keep doing what you must to keep your body and connections healthy, but give all your remaining attention to the mind & emotions and spirit pillars with the aim of strengthening those areas.

In an upcoming chapter, I'll talk about how to do this even when you have absolutely no time.

First, let's get clear on which self-care practices actually build strong pillars. I don't know about you, but I don't have a lot of time or energy, so I need whatever I do to be as impactful as possible.

Choosing Self-Care Tasks Wisely

How do we select self-care tasks that will actually work for us? Let's look at our ingredients again. We need something that promotes honesty, trust, respect, and open communication. Where all that honesty, trust, respect, and open communication is directed will depend on which pillar we're applying it to.

What body activity could you do that would require you to be honest with your body, trusting of your body, respectful of your body, all while teaching you to communicate with your body?

Go on and ask yourself. Maybe journal about it. I'll wait. I'm not in a hurry here. This time is for you. Do what you gotta do and then come back when you're ready.

What did you come up with?

Yoga, maybe? Martial arts, perhaps? Long walks? Learning how to eat healthy or find exercise that you love, that your body enjoys doing?

Same question, but now consider the mind & emotions. Journaling teaches us honesty and communication. Therapy, too. Or AA (in any of the anonymouses, you'll find lots of advocacy for honesty, trust, respect, and open communication).

The spirit pillar asks that we do tasks that prioritize our joy, those big feelings of awe, spiritual connection (if we're into that), that we look for a job that lights us up if ours is sucking us dry. That we use our creativity and imagination and play.

Connection requires that we get real up close and comfortable with feelings of vulnerability. Making friends, setting boundaries. *Yes*, setting boundaries and saying no are self-care tasks.

In all cases, not only do you want to consider all four pillars, and how to apply honesty, trust, respect, and open communications to those areas of your life, but there's also the holy trinity to consider.

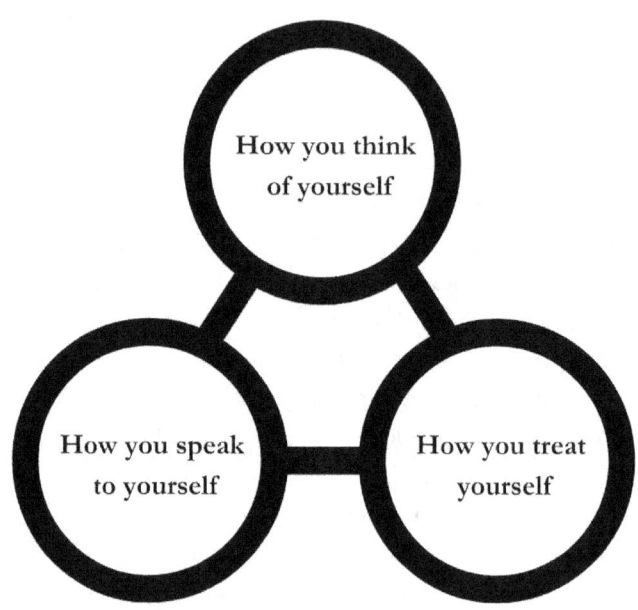

Foundation of Wellbeing

The holy trinity accounts for our thoughts, speech, and actions. How you think of yourself, how you speak about yourself, and how you act toward yourself. Remember that we want the relationship with ourselves to be friendly. We can't achieve that if we don't treat ourselves well in thought, speech, and action.

But maybe this is still too vague. Let's go deeper.

In fact, let's take the pillars one by one, and see what self-care with a focus on relationship-building might look like in practice.

. . .

Body Pillar Self-Care
Examples: martial arts, yoga, cooking, sleep, exercise, body work, body care

A little less than a year after my mother's brain injury, I moved to Michigan for school. It was here that I began studying Uechi-Ryu, a Japanese style of martial arts that focuses on body conditioning.

By the time I earned my black belt, my confidence in my ability to protect myself had grown significantly. This was the first time in my life that I felt safe in my body after a lifetime of hypervigilance created by the constant threat of violence.

Martial arts was a good body pillar self-care task for me because it cultivated positive feelings toward my body and its abilities. It changed how I thought of myself, how I spoke about myself, and how I acted toward myself.

Exercise was also a good body pillar activity because not only did it improve my health, but it also helped to stabilize my moods.

Some days I would rather stab myself with a fork (or better yet, some dumplings) than exercise, but I will admit that I *always* feel better after I do.

The key to choosing a body pillar task is choosing something that cultivates positive feelings toward yourself. If it's motiving to feel your body get stronger through exercise, or you're really proud that your cooking skills are improving, if baking gives you joy, or you're so glad you finally invested in that new mattress because you're sleeping so much better—whatever it is, feeling proud of yourself is one of the signs that you're on track.

Feeling good about your body and the choices you make will motivate you to keep making them. Contrarily, if the self-care task detracts from your sense of pride or self-love, it's probably not the best activity for you.

That's why I stopped weighing myself and even told my doctor to stop telling me the number as well. Part of connecting with my body was learning to value how I felt *in* my body and listening to what *it* told me over what some scale had to say. This helped me to repair my relationship with my body. I almost never weigh myself anymore. It's not good for my mental health.

Flexibility is also needed when we are working on our relationship with our bodies.

Your relationship with your body will change over time because our bodies are always changing, but you can still have a great relationship with your body despite its shifting circumstances.

I no longer do martial arts, for example. Too many injuries and carelessness have encouraged me to seek out gentler forms of exertion. Now I prefer long walks and yoga. I also enjoy strength training and will do it as my back allows.

It's possible you will need to change your self-care tasks to meet yourself where you are at any given time in your life. It might help to view this as a chance to practice honesty with yourself.

You haven't forgotten about honesty, trust, respect, and open communication, have you? Because it's important for the body self-care tasks too. Being honest with where we are, trusting our bodies, respecting them and listening to them—all of that should be present and accounted for no matter what self-care task we choose.

Yoga taught me how to listen to what my body was telling me and to respect what my body can and can't do. True, I blackened my eye doing crow pose once, when I rolled too far forward and slammed my face against the wooden floor of the studio in a room full of people.

This was made worse when my friend rushed to my side and dramatically cried out, "Oh my god, are you okay?"

This likely ruined the vibe that the teacher had tried to achieve with the low lights and soft music and incense, but hey, these things happen. You, too, might humiliate yourself in a room full of strangers someday. If you haven't already.

It's all part of the experience of finding our limitations. We must find them before we can practice accepting them.

The art of loving your body is about showing it as much grace and kindness as it needs. Whatever helps you to achieve that is on the table. That said, there are a few standards for everyone: sleeping, eating.

But there is a difference in meeting your basic needs with an attitude that your body is an inescapable nuisance and being deeply grateful for all the pleasure and experience you gain from it.

I find this challenging when my back is really hurting. Some days it feels like the pain will never go away, which can feed a feeling of hopelessness. When this happens, I have to remind myself to keep the commitment of thinking, speaking, and acting lovingly toward myself.

I also want to acknowledge that if you have a high-maintenance body, it might be more challenging to love your body. Health conditions and physical impairments can make it harder to love a body. In that case, it may help to find someone with your condition(s) who can model for you what a loving relationship with themselves even in the presence of those specific challenges looks like.

The world is full of inspiring people who give us the courage and strength to go on. Finding yourself a hero might inspire you to heal your relationship with your body and give you a focal point even on the most challenging days.

Sometimes the damage we do to our bodies is self-inflicted, and we have to learn to forgive ourselves for that.

In my case, in order to heal my relationship with my body, I needed to first overcome my disordered eating, which vacillated between anorexia and bulimia. I had to learn how to shift my focus and goals from what I looked like to what would nourish me, what I enjoyed, what made me happy.

I found the most success by learning to focus on what I *wanted* rather than what I was trying to avoid. For example, my family's medical history puts me at a higher risk for heart problems and arthritis, but I *want* a healthy heart and bones that don't ache. So I don't eat meat and I limit dairy and eggs to keep my cholesterol down. I try to limit sugar and eat more ginger and anti-inflammatories for my bones, especially my finnicky back. When it comes to fruits and veggies, I try to eat all the colors in a day. This is an easy way to make sure I'm getting a variety of vitamins and minerals in my diet.

By focusing on something like colors and variety, I can make sure I'm thinking about nutrition and not numbers on a scale. If the number on a scale doesn't negatively affect your relationship with yourself, by all means use it. But if seeing a number makes you feel bad about yourself, or triggers a self-punishing spiral, maybe it's time to put the scale away and find a new way to measure your progress.

Choose body pillar tasks that give you energy, build confidence in your abilities, and make you feel great about yourself. Make sure your focus and effort aren't being invested in unrealistic expectations for yourself and how your body *should* be.

Focus instead on accepting, enjoying, and appreciating your body as it is now. The condition of your body will change. Unconditional love for your body will require that you love it even when it's not working so well. That's why any self-care task that helps you to build gratitude for your body—no matter how imperfect it may be—is a big win.

Health is an incredible blessing, but some of us will never be healthy. So please know that if you're not healthy, you can still have a good relationship with your body.

Mind & Emotions Pillar Self-Care Examples

Examples: meditation, mindfulness, therapy, breathwork, journaling, affirmations

When meditation was first recommended to me, I thought it was a joke even though it was at the end of a yoga class. If anyone was going to meditate, it'd be these people. I was told to sit down, get comfortable, and see what came up.

Excuse me?

See what came up? No need, good sir. I was *very* aware of what would come up.

I'd had several years of therapy under my belt at this point.

Like most traumatized people, I was still dealing with strong emotional reactivity. To be highly emotionally reactive is the opposite of being emotionally regulated. Let's use the metaphor of emotional regulation as volume control. [7] When you are emotionally reactive, the volume is way up. Even the smallest stressor can feel like a major crisis when emotions are on full blast. Emotional regulation is learning to turn the volume on your emotions down.

But emotional regulation becomes difficult when chronically exposed to trauma and neglect as a child.

Thanks, Mom. Thanks, Dad.

Because meditation was supposed to be a very effective way to develop emotional regulation skills, and because I was absolutely sick of being enslaved by my emotions, I was ready to try just about anything to be free of them. But I was still highly skeptical.

When I thought of meditation I thought of Buddhists in their little robes, looking serene. I saw nothing of myself in all of that.

Worse, I once had a panic attack while trying to meditate. A panic attack! I thought meditation was supposed to cure intense emotions.

It took me a while to realize that the panic I was feeling during meditation was my mind's overreaction to playing with the volume button. I finally found the volume button and started to turn it down, and the mind gremlin was like, *Holy hell, what are you doing? You can't turn my volume down! How will you hear me? What if there's danger? What if something catastrophic is about to happen and you can't even hear the alarm bells?*

Cue the panic.

These initial spikes of strong emotion and overwhelm are part of learning how to regulate. That's why I recommend having a good therapist, or a sponsor, for this part of the pillar-building experience.

Therapy is a great way to get to know your thoughts and feelings, but so are meditation, mindfulness, journaling, and visualization.

Our minds and our emotions control how we see ourselves and the world and how we react to everything that happens. It has tremendous power over us for that reason.

That's why when we stroll into the little ol' town of mind & emotions and declare there is a new sheriff, we can expect a showdown in the street. Our thoughts and feelings will not give up without a fight. They like being in charge. They're power hungry and have gotten really comfortable holding the reins. That's why I say there's no shame in getting professional help here, because sometimes it's best to have backup if we're going to challenge the world order, or at the very least, *our* world order.

Spirit Pillar Self-Care Examples

Examples: creativity, play, joy, meaningful work, adventuring, learning new things, service, spiritual practices

It's hard to describe what being connected to your spirit feels like if you've never experienced it, or at least, didn't recognize it for what it was when it happened. But here are a few moments when I felt my spirit wake up.

When looking at the night sky. The glimpse of a full moon through bare tree branches. Or all those visible stars over a quiet desert landscape. After reading a poem, lowering the book to savor the silent music of it ringing through me. At parties (yes, even us introverts go to parties), in an unexpected moment when I look up and see a room full of people I care about, laughing, smiling, and having a good time. After all those years on my own, can you imagine what that felt like for me?

Or when I lie on my back in the grass and watch the clouds pass by. When a brilliant idea has come to me on one of my long, leisurely walks and I rush home, excited to the gills, to write it down before I forget. The first time I saw the goddess of victory alighting on a warship in the Louvre. To think all of those incredible details of her body and the folds of her billowing clothes are made of *stone*.

Someone made that out of a rock! Are you *kidding* me?

When I see someone act so beautifully brave it brings me to tears. Like when people rush in to help and protect others in dangerous situations, when they probably want to—and should—run away in fear. When I hear a good song, or watch a good movie, or connect to any story that stirs something up in me. Being reunited with a good friend, or my love, after time apart.

I hope you can see how impossible my task is here—trying to describe the ineffable.

I wish for everyone that our connection to ourselves is always clear and bright. But for someone like me—and perhaps you too—loss can dull our shine. This is even more true when those negative experiences are chronic. Whatever lit us up before becomes more like a lit candle thrown down a very deep, very dark well. A brief flicker and nothing more.

For me, reconnecting with my spirit was two-fold.

On one hand, it was about untangling the binds on my creativity that I'd invertedly created when I became a full-time author. When I kept writing more and more to the fans' expectations and less for my own satisfaction, I started to burn out.

Many artists and creatives have talked about the metaphor of the creative well.

So much so, I'm not even sure who to credit for the idea (sorry about that). But the idea is that you have to put more water into this well than you pull out, or your well will go dry.

Hence the burnout.

Because I certainly drew from my well faster than I could refill it. When my writing career became about making everyone else happy, I lost my way. But what could I do? I was trying to pay the bills, so it was an honest mistake to make.

Or we can think of the spirit as flame.

Like any fire, we have to feed it, or it will go out.

But figuring out what feeds the flame is tricky. I listed some of my favorites: time in nature, writing, viewing art, adventuring with friends, reading. Baking. Having a think.

What about you?

Were there games you loved as a kid before the world forced you to grow up? This is a good place to start because I've found we often have similar interests even as adults. I was insane for my Teddy Ruxpin doll because it would read me stories on cassette tapes. My art interests were reflected in my coloring, painting, Lite Brite, and spiral stencil set. I also wore out an Easy-Bake Oven. I ate more cheese pizzas through the BOOK-IT! reading program than I have in all the other remaining years of my life combined. I loved all the spooky stories written by the likes of R. L. Stein and Christopher Pike. So unsurprisingly, I found great joy in making a fun little ghost story. Cold Shoulder: A Ghost Story is an eight-minute audio drama that I wrote, produced, and put up for free on my YouTube channel for Halloween.

I had no expectations for it, only a desire to indulge in my love of all things spooky.

So if you're lost on what lights you up, start by making a review of what you did as a kid. If you don't remember, look through old photos if you can.

If that's a no go, let's consider anything that makes you laugh, makes you think, makes you go outside. Reading Julia Cameron's *The Artist's Way* might also shake some ideas loose. Or pay attention to what you can't shut up about. Is there a topic that really gets you going?

There are also spiritual practices. Building a relationship with God (whatever that means for you) can bring back the light. If you're not into God, the other suggestions still apply.

What could someone be talking about that would make you sit up and pay attention? What interests you? What delights you?

Have fun with this. Take your time. If you have no idea what lights you up, try everything. You might surprise yourself. We should all be open to trying new things anyway, as our tastes can change.

What I advise you not to do is what I am often guilty of doing: overcomplication.

I take what should be fun and enjoyable and turn it into work.

Are you also guilty of taking things too seriously?

This is usually how it goes for me.

Let's say someone asks me to make a cake for a party because I have decent baking skills. I say yes, because why not? Who doesn't love baking a cake for a friend? Except that now I've started thinking about how everyone at the party is going to see this cake, not just my friend. They're going to taste it too. This leads me to conclude that I'll definitely be judged on how it turns out.

As a result I decide I have to do an amazing job or everyone will think I'm the most talentless baker in the land, and possibly stop liking me altogether.

I get everything together—including some fancy pans and tools I bought but didn't need for this cake, just so I could level up my finished project. I set off to design a cake that will blow minds in both appearance and taste.

Before I know it, I've watched a hundred videos on how to make a cake properly—as if I didn't know before—and I've made two, possibly three trips to the store to get everything I need to execute this rapidly escalating vision.

Now, because I've tried to execute a vision too ambitious for my skillset, of course it comes out imperfectly. I try again. When I still can't produce a cake gorgeous enough to erase all my fear of judgment and crushing perfectionist tendencies (which no cake will achieve unless perhaps I am named star baker of the week on *Great British Bake Off*), I will feel worse about myself than ever.

By the end, the stress and pressure will be so high I can't possibly enjoy the task I usually take pleasure in (making cakes) because I've added too much to the equation.

I do this all the time—take things that I love and turn them into an odyssey.

I add pressure and unrealistic expectations and goals.

Then when I finally present my little cake to my friend, she might say, "You did too much! I was just thinking of the simple chocolate one you made for my birthday last year. I loved it."

I'm left to wonder why I put myself through all that. Again.

I'm also guilty of turning my back on play altogether because I'm too busy being a *sensible* adult. An adult who pays her bills and her taxes—granted I'm always drenched in fear that I'm doing it wrong and will be carried off to debtor's prison. (The internet assures me it was abolished in 1833.)

I might tell myself I don't have time to do the things I love. And if I do it anyway, I'll feel guilty about it the entire time, wondering why I'm not getting my work done instead.

This is something we could stand to unlearn.

Play is doing things you love because you're lucky enough to have the chance to do them. You only have a little time on this planet, so why not see, do, and experience as much of it as you can?

Why can't we simply be here in the present moment, relishing every second of this miracle called life?

Because we have bills and responsibilities. And a thousand domestic problems to solve.

That's why.

That's also why we do jobs we don't love, so we can pay those bills. The more and more we run on this hamster wheel of deprioritizing our well-being for the well-being of others, the farther and farther we get away from true contentment.

Another issue is that I never liked the word *contentment*. In French, it literally means *happy*. Je suis contente. *I am happy.* For a long time, I thought it translated to *I am content*.

How underwhelming.

What I really mean by content is that feeling that everything is okay. You're not worried about the bills and how things are going to work out for you. You're not waiting for some imaginary puzzle piece to click into place so you can enjoy your life. You're at peace with the way things are *now*, even if they don't look the way you thought they would.

How do we create this magical feeling of contentment?

By indulging in play, cultivating joy, and prioritizing our happiness because we know that nothing we do is going to change the fact that we don't have a lot of time on this Earth. Our lives will be over before we know it.

Holding that truth at the forefront of the mind will allow us to maintain the perspective that we need.

Easier said than done, of course.

I never feel less relaxed than when I'm *trying* to have a good time.

Because the truth is that I've become more comfortable with working than I am with relaxing.

Why? Because I have more practice working. I have more positive reinforcement such as praise or achievement. No one ever tells me how amazing I am when I take a day off. Then there's the financial payoff itself, of course. All of that seems more exciting than *resting*.

But play is needed to fill me up with well water or flame or whatever else I might need to prevent burnout. It fulfills a vital role in our well-being, which is why it has a pillar of its very own.

Choose self-care tasks that lessen your resistance to joy and play. Tasks that cultivate a feeling of peace and contentment. Even if in the beginning, you do those tasks thinking about what a sensible adult you are and how sensible adults really need to be filing their taxes instead.

If you need permission, by the way, you have it. I, Kory, give you permission to go play.

Often and in whatever fashion makes your heart sing.

Purpose and Meaning

Perhaps this section should be called Spirit Pillar Examples Part II. I say this because while using our creativity, spending time in nature, delighting in small things, having a gratitude practice, or exploring our relationship with God/Universe/Source (if we want) are all ways to fill ourselves up, there is also another way.

By creating purpose.

Recently I gave a keynote presentation to a room full of lovely health care professionals at their annual spring conference. In preparing for presentations, I always try to tailor my talks to that specific audience as much as possible. In order to do that, for weeks beforehand, I start reading about that industry's pain points and struggles.

What I discovered during this bout of research is that health care professionals have a high rate of burning out due to their constant exposure to a high-demand, low-resource environment. They are asked to accomplish a lot with very little support. We could certainly say that they are pulling water from the well faster than it can be replenished. They often develop chronic pain—with which I can deeply sympathize—due to lifting and supporting patients. But one of the single most protective factors against burnout is finding meaning and purpose [8] in one's work.

But what does that even mean? To find meaning and purpose in one's work?

I asked myself this question a lot when my mother died. Writing *Who Killed My Mother?* gave me an excuse to do a postmortem on her life—and mine. My mother died at fifty-six years old, about one month before her birthday.

When we lose someone we love unexpectedly, nonsensically, it's easy to think that life has no meaning. Why did all those terrible things happen to her? Why did all those terrible things happen to me? What was the purpose of it all?

I was looking for answers somewhere *out there* to make sense of the situation, but really I was looking in the wrong place.

The only one who can assign meaning and purpose to my life is me.

Sometimes we think of purpose as this grand notion. And that it must be given to us by some power greater than ourselves. God, perhaps. An angel, maybe. At the very least a community who is entrusting us with a sacred mission for the good of all.

That's *purpose*.

But we can give ourselves purpose.

I do so by transmuting my experiences into a source of light. And you can too.

Whatever has happened to you, no matter how wretched, you can use *anything* that's happened to you and make it meaningful.

Here are some examples:

My childhood was difficult and left me with a lot to heal. That *means* I can share my healing techniques and help as many people as I can.

My mother was murdered by her abusive brother. That *means* I understand abuse dynamics and can use my knowledge to show others how to safeguard their own well-being.

I survived narcissistic abuse. That *means* I can show others how to spot manipulation and clean up the mental mess such abuse creates.

And they don't all have to be negatives to positives either. Here is a positive-to-positive example:

I'm passionate about books and stories. That *means* I can use stories to change how people think and to add more joy and fun to their days.

Any of these statements also work with the word *purpose*.

It's my purpose to help others heal.

It's my purpose to advocate for our collective well-being.

It's my purpose to tell stories and help others rewrite theirs.

The important takeaway here is that you are the one who gets to assign meaning to your life, your experiences, and your work.

You.

That's your power and your right. No one needs to tell you that the work you do is valuable and worthy. It's nice when people do that, of course. Don't think I don't love it when someone tells me they like my books. But if someone tells me it's shit, I try not to take that to heart.

But give your life and your experiences meaning and purpose. Even if the meaning is, "My life has no grand meaning. I'm only meant to enjoy my time here. My purpose is joy and not taking something like meaning and purpose too seriously."

Excellent. If that works for you, that's good with me.

Whatever you want to do with your life, do it. Just make sure that it's really what *you* value. Because spending your precious time on this Earth doing what everyone else thinks is meaningful and purposeful is a fantastic way to waste your life.

Connection Pillar Self-Care Examples

Examples: building community, making friends, practicing vulnerability, romance, getting out of your comfort zone, setting boundaries

I've said it before and I'll say it again, connection is a tough one for me. I know it's valuable and I know I need it, but people are *wild*. It felt very unsafe to put myself out there to meet people, make friends, find the love of my life, or create a found family. It felt even more unsafe than trying to hold my bomb blast of a family together with nothing more than a frayed rubber band and a couple of paper clips. At least I knew how my family would act. With strangers, I never knew what to expect.

But I am forever grateful that I did find it in me to hope for more. Few things have been more healing in my life than finding people who really love me for who I am. It's true that I was very suspicious of other people's affections for a long time. Frankly I still am with anyone new.

Yet unconditional love was so different than anything I had experienced before. With conditional love there were always boxes that had to be checked, criteria that had to be met, and love that had to be earned before I could receive an ounce of the affection owed to every child.

Unconditional love begins within us. How can we expect other people to love and support us unconditionally, without reservation, when we can't do that for ourselves?

But finding people who love you unconditionally can teach you a lot about how to love yourself unconditionally too. These souls can mirror your worth back to you, shift your assessment of yourself, and provide new perspectives, assuming you are open to the praise.

This love, however, is not a replacement for self-love. But it can be a sturdy stepping-stone to it. The good news is that your self-love will naturally develop as you invest in your pillars. You don't have to set out to self-love yourself exactly. By building the pillars and implementing the policies of honesty, trust, respect, and open communication, self-love will grow. Even more so if you clean up the way you think, speak, and act toward yourself.

That still leaves us with making external connections.

For me, making connections is kind of like working out. I am never excited to do it, but once it's done, I'm always glad I went.

It's important to point out here that the number of people in your life is less important than the closeness and health of those connections. Quality, not quantity, is what we're looking for here.

Connecting with others is one self-care practice in this pillar, but so is setting boundaries. Drawing clear lines in the sand regarding what behaviors are and aren't acceptable in your present relationships. In fact, if you don't already have boundaries in all of your relationships, I would say this is the most important self-care technique you could employ in this pillar.

Set boundaries.

For many of us, it can be intimidating to do so, but they really are in the best interests of everyone involved.

There are three moments in my life when I remember setting firm boundaries that caused big shifts for me.

When I left my mother at the end of my grandmother's driveway even though I was terrified I was leaving her to die, that was the first time I did what I knew was best for my own healing and well-being. As hard as it was, that was a big moment for me.

The second time I set a useful boundary was when I forced myself into that stint of celibacy because I didn't trust myself to be around anyone pretty and also keep a single thought to my own health in my head at the same time, at least not until I built up my own willpower substantially.

I spent the night in the trunk of a car, remember!

The third boundary was with my father, when I decided to go no contact with him, as many other children of narcissists are forced to do when they realize their narcissistic parent has no interest in changing their behavior and never will. As long as you are within reach, the abuse will continue.

In regard to my father, the final insult was a text telling me that he'd heard about my mother's death. Of course I had not told him myself. I had been forced to listen to him degrade my mother all my childhood, and after losing her, I didn't want or need his opinion on what had happened. His response to her death in the text only confirmed what I'd expected from him.

Your mother's death was a long time coming. She has no one to blame but herself.

Not "Are you okay?"

Not "Do you need anything?"

His complete lack of awareness regarding my pain in the situation made it very clear to me that he neither had nor was capable of compassion and empathy for me.

And when people show us that they have no compassion, respect, or empathy for us, it is best to put a firm boundary in place. Or perhaps an impenetrable steel wall.

Boundaries will be different for everyone because we all need different things. Perhaps you hate deception, and therefore you have a boundary around lying.

Maybe you were screamed at a lot as a kid and now you have a boundary around yelling as an adult. That's your call to make because if you know that being yelled at by someone will trigger and upset you,

you have every right to set a boundary about the acceptable volume that can be used in arguments.

I should also mention that boundaries are fluid. You may need a boundary around something today in order to protect your well-being but later discover that once you've healed, you don't need to be so protective of that part of you anymore.

Or the fluidity might be attached to the closeness of the connection. Maybe with your acquaintances you have more relaxed boundaries until you get to know them better. Or firmer boundaries with your family who you know quite well.

In addition to boundaries, the connection pillar is about doing what you can to keep your heart soft. Connecting is risky, but in my opinion, it's a risk worth taking.

Many of us were deeply hurt in our connections. A love relationship could end in the most spectacular way. We lose a friend. We have to cut off some or all of our family. That disappointment really takes a toll on our heart. The natural reaction to disappointment is to shut down and grow distant.

In fact, they may even—inaccurately—say they're just setting a boundary.

But I have to say, it's not a boundary if it's bitter. Resentful. If it's hateful. It's not a boundary if you put it up like a stone wall on all sides to protect yourself from the big bad world.

A boundary is meant to keep you safe and well, absolutely. It's not, however, supposed to be an attempt to force the world into a shape you can stand. All that will do is make your life so small, so cramped, that you will walk around inside it feeling as if you are suffocating.

Boundaries must be balanced with optimism. If you're optimistic that you'll find everything you need in your connections—people who love you unconditionally, stand by you unconditionally, and mirror your best qualities back to you when you can't even do that for yourself—and you have boundaries in place to guide those relationships to their fullest potential, then you'll be right there in that sweet spot.

I know what I'm asking of you.

I really do.

I can't tell you how hard it was to hold space in my heart for the dream that one day love and acceptance—in any form whatsoever—would come back into my life after so much betrayal.

For a long time, there wasn't anyone in my life I could point to and say, "See, that person is different. They love me for who I am. They don't want anything from me."

I had only the hope that it might be true.

Someday.

If by chance you are in the same dark place, then this is a big ask, I know.

But I have to ask anyway.

Please have hope.

Have hope that things will get better even if you have no evidence in your life that it could possibly happen for you.

Believe anyway.

Believe until the dream comes true.

Key Chapter Takeaways

- Your well-being is a relationship that you build with yourself. Self-care tasks are the activities you complete in order to build that relationship.
- The best self-care tasks are those that nurture honesty, trust, respect, and open communication.
- Our relationship with ourselves will be its strongest if all four areas—body, mind & emotions, spirit, and connection—are equally well cared for.
- Don't worry about self-love. It will develop naturally as you work on your four pillars and how you think, speak, and act toward yourself.
- Only you can decide which self-care strategies are best for you, given your current needs, interests, and where you are in your healing.
- Your needs will change with time and circumstance. Adjust accordingly.

THE MOST USEFUL SIDE EFFECT OF SELF-CARE: RESILIENCY

Life is hard. You know that. I know that. My dog who believes he hasn't had enough treats today knows that. (He has had *so* many.)

What makes life not so hard is resiliency. Resiliency can take a mountain and shrink it to a molehill. The only problem is that none of us really *enjoy* the resiliency-building process.

Traditionally, humans have become resilient by overcoming difficulty.

Bad things happen. We overcome them or we die.

The good news: you don't have to go looking for challenges in life in order to increase your resiliency. The bad news: the challenges will find *you*.

If you've ever felt like you were unwillingly subscribed to God's strongest-soldier plan, you're probably intimately acquainted with this kind of suffering already. In this arena, we're forced to navigate whichever disaster shows up: a dysfunctional family, a cheating spouse, unemployment, crushing debt, failure, disappointment, a lost friend, an illness, or the death of someone we love.

These normal and seemingly all-too-frequent life events will come whether we like it or not, and despite our best efforts, overcoming tragedy will make us stronger.

Or we can build our resiliency a different way.

Can you guess what that way is?

Yes! By healing your relationship with yourself, by investing in the four pillars through the use of self-care that builds the skills of honesty, trust, respect, and open communication.

This entire book, if you haven't noticed, is my pitch for why you should prioritize this relationship rather than just letting life run you through the wringer every time your number comes up.

Remember the story I told you in the beginning about how my mother and I both had high trauma scores but our lives looked very different?

Resiliency is why. I am more resilient than my mother was.

Resilience is our ability to adapt, recover, and bounce back from the hard stuff. It's our capacity to withstand and navigate difficult or stressful situations, and to emerge stronger, more capable, and more resourceful as a result.

Investing in my relationship with myself not only helped me to heal everything that had happened, thereby weakening the effects the trauma had on me, but it also helped to future-proof me against forthcoming challenges.

Can we eliminate hardship altogether? I wish.

It's hard to hear, but no one on this planet will achieve the perfect life.

Never.

No matter what you do or who you become.

No matter how rich, how powerful, how beautiful, or loved you are, you will not achieve the unachievable.

And a perfect life is certainly unachievable.

Steve Jobs was one of the richest men on Earth, and he still died of pancreatic cancer. He still struggled in his relationships. He still had his company snatched out from underneath him. This tells us that there is no amount of money or power in this world to protect us from the trials of life.

Old age, heartache, illness, and eventually death will come for even the most fortunate of us.

This may be hard to hear, that difficulty comes for us all.

I struggled with this myself for a long time. And sometimes I still do.

I held fast to the belief that if I *just* worked hard enough, did all the right things, accomplished enough, and prepared enough, then surely *I* would be the exception. *I* would find a way to eliminate misfortune.

If there was a way, believe me, I would have found it. I have left no stone unturned.

And while I did not find the perfection I was hoping for, what I did find was that by investing in my relationship with myself rather than focusing on avoiding suffering at all costs, I found the relief I was hoping for.

If we can't achieve a perfect life through self-care, what can we achieve? What's the actual payoff for building this relationship with ourselves? What are we even doing it for?

For the resilience.

Resilience is the big payoff of self-care.

People have called me resilient because—and I quote—"Look at everything that happened to you and yet you didn't break."

Usually this is when I begin to wonder if they had been listening to me at all because I thought I had been *abundantly* clear that my experiences *did* break me. I felt completely broken when I was suicidal, bulimic, racked with self-loathing, drowning in shame, single, friendless, depressed, lonely, and anxious.

It's true that I'm harder to break *now*. But that wasn't always the case. And I want you to know that it doesn't have to be the case for you either. If you just so happened to pick up this book when you were, in fact, feeling pretty damn broken, that's okay.

Broken is a great place to start.

We can work with broken.

When we are at the starting line of "broken," we have a lot of options. We can repair the damage done. Or we choose to see this as a fresh start and a chance to build a life better suited for us.

You don't have to be superhuman to begin this work.

You don't even have to have an ounce of resilience to your name.

Resilience will develop naturally as you craft the tools you need to build that relationship with yourself.

But I just wanted to make it clear that seeking perfection in life is a fool's errand.

You can be perfect or you can be free.

And I really want freedom for you.

Part of that freedom comes from letting go of the notion that we can move through life without being impacted by it.

Consider the big, ancient, and beautiful moon in our night sky. It is full of craters for a reason—we live in a universe of impacts. Even the Earth has hundreds of crater lakes.

Impacts, I'm sorry to say, are inevitable. They happen all the time.

You and I, like everyone else, are going to take our share of hits.

We can freak out about this (as I certainly have). Or we can invest in our resiliency, so the impacts don't feel quite *so* impactful. In reality, we most often do a bit of both.

The stronger your relationship with yourself, the greater your ability to turn a mountain into a molehill when disaster strikes.

Unpleasant experiences are always easier to endure when we have a great friend at our side to face the dangers and difficulties with us.

What I'm trying to say with all of this is that it will feel like you always have that brave, funny, honest, trustworthy friend at your side if you become that friend to yourself.

We build that friendship by spending time with ourselves and by investing in joy, meditation, journaling, affirmations, therapy, exercise, sleep, rest, self-care, strong bonds with others, boundaries, connecting with meaning and purpose, gratitude, and courage.

Of course, self-care tasks teach us more than resiliency.

If you practice meditation, which teaches patience, then you will naturally be more patient when your coworker brings the bullshit to the next Monday-morning meeting.

If you practice joy, you will be more hopeful and optimistic when an obstacle pops up, rather than tumble into a spiral.

If you develop self-awareness through mindfulness practices, you'll be quicker at recognizing when you're knocked off balance. When you're about to say the mean thing or make the situation worse.

If you develop a flexible mindset, you'll be more adaptable in the face of change and more comfortable with the uncertainties of life that we all face.

If you connect with meaning and purpose, you will have a sense of direction and a target to focus on that align with your values and thereby are less likely to be disrupted by the natural fluctuations of life.

If you learn to regulate your emotions when the tension and pressure are high, you'll be better equipped to deal with stress and problems.

If you can see your negative experiences as a learning opportunity, and mine those moments for wisdom and insight, you will always gain more than you lose from any situation—no matter how dire.

I could go on for days with the examples, and I've tried in my podcast *A Well Cared For Human*, which has over one hundred episodes as I write this, but you get the point.

Build your pillars and the resiliency will come.

Key Chapter Takeaways

- Resilience refers to mental, emotional, and physical fortitude. The more resilient we are, the easier it is to cope with difficulties.
- Resilience is the big payoff of self-care.
- Self-care builds the pillars. The stronger the pillars, the stronger our resilience.
- No one will achieve a perfect life free of loss and disappointment. It is better to live freely than perfectly.

MOST COMMON SELF-CARE BARRIER: "I DON'T HAVE TIME."

One of the most common complaints I hear about self-care is this: "I don't have time."

It doesn't matter how we actually express this: "I'm too busy. I'm too stressed. By the end of the day, I'm too tired. I can't imagine possibly squeezing even thirty more seconds out of my day to make room for this."

No matter how it is phrased, these words highlight the same erroneous belief that we need a lot of time to practice self-care.

It's true that if you *have* more time to spend on self-care, that would be time well spent. But if you don't have a lot of time, that doesn't mean there is no hope for you.

Some of us simply have more responsibility and more demands on our time.

When that's the case, we have to learn how to catch our breath while running.

I learned this phrase from my friend Joe.

Joe was my hairdresser in graduate school, and briefly, also my running coach. He was a great runner. I was not. I was just a girl in her twenties trying to heal her relationship with her body and conquer an eating disorder.

I'd broken my bulimia cycle, but now I was trying to figure out what I could do with all those impulses. Go for a run, was what I'd decided on. As a middle-aged woman with chronic back pain this sounds incomprehensible to me now, but at the time I thought it was a brilliant idea.

And it worked. In part because I had support from helpful people like Joe.

One day while running with Joe, who was coaching me on my form, I was complaining that my pace was too slow and that I was too out of breath to speed up. In response he dropped this gold nugget of wisdom: "You can slow down as much as you need to, but don't stop."

I will say the same to you now. Slow down your life as much as you need to, but don't stop.

Don't stop taking care of yourself.

Don't stop loving yourself.

Don't give up on yourself or the vision you have for your life.

There will simply be times when the demands are too high and the pressure too great for us to take care of ourselves. When this happens, there's still a lot we can do.

Learn to catch your breath while running.

My top tactics for self-care when time is slim on the ground are:

1. Boundaries
2. Simplification
3. Breathing techniques
4. Mindfulness
5. Mental de-escalation

There is no special order here. It just depends on what you need given your situation. Let's take them one by one.

Boundaries

First and foremost, if you don't have time to take care of yourself, please start saying no more. Seriously, stop saying yes to things. You don't have time to say yes unless it's something that brings you absolute joy. If so, keep doing it because cultivating joy is self-care. That's the spirit pillar, remember?

When you start saying no to all incoming requests, it's possible that you will experience some pushback. This is especially true if the people making demands of your time are used to getting a yes out of you.

If they ask for something, you say, "Sorry, I can't," and they reply, "Oh, okay. Is everything all right?" then this is a good friend. They didn't push. They respected your needs. They are now concerned for your well-being because they recognize that you usually are a helper when able. Keep them.

If, however, you say no and they keep pushing, you can try the following script:

You: "I'm sorry, I can't do that. I'm overwhelmed at the moment."

Them: "Why? Come on. It'll only take five minutes."

If you're a smart ass like me, you'd say, "Then do it yourself if it's only five minutes." If you're nicer, you might say, "I would if I could, but it's just not possible right now. Sorry."

Them: "Wow, okay. I just thought I could count on you for this. I mean, after everything I did for you…"

This is what boundary violation looks like. This person is disrespecting your time and needs, and worse, they're trying to use guilt and pressure to get a certain behavior out of you.

This is manipulative.

There are many ways you can work with manipulation and boundary violation. I recommend that you be as direct and firm as possible. Some people just don't get boundaries. Being direct and firm is the best way to handle such people.

How you choose to be direct is up to you. And yes, I am very aware that being direct is very hard for many of us—myself included—especially if we've been raised to be polite and accommodating. If you have boundary-violating family members when boundaries weren't even allowed, when you dared try to enforce one, they'd act like you broke a solemn vow.

Here are some ways you be direct but firm:

With kindness: "I can see you really want me to do this, but I'm sorry, I can't. I'd love to help you if I could."

With a focus on self-respect: "I can see you really want me to do this, but you're making me uncomfortable, when you're trying to force me to do something I don't want to do."

With sarcasm: "I'd rather not. Thanks."

With a hint of aggression: "I can see you really want me to do this, but why can't you do it for yourself? Are you saying your time is more valuable than *mine*?"

Firm with no embellishments: "No. I don't want to."

Or with this simple, complete sentence: "No."

You don't owe anyone any explanations or reasons. Your desire to not do it is enough, and it should be for them as well. Often we think we are the rude person for refusing to help, but in truth, they are being rude when they don't respect your time and boundaries.

If they have all kinds of feelings about your boundaries, that is their work, not yours.

I once went out to dinner with friends of my friend. There were four or five of us, including my friend and me. At the end of the meal, everyone started hugging goodbye.

I hugged everyone even though I don't really like to hug strangers. I told myself it was okay because these were friends of my friends. Then I got to the last girl and she stopped me.

"Sorry, but I don't hug people I don't know well," she said.

I was so surprised, I didn't immediately react. I think I just stood there, my arms half lifted in the unfinished hug.

"I can see I disappointed you," she said. "Sorry about that. It's not personal."

"It's okay," I said. "Don't worry about it."

But she was right. I'd never had anyone *refuse* a hug before, let alone in a group of huggers. She hugged everyone but me, so I couldn't help but feel rejected.

But those feelings were my problem, not hers. She had a boundary, and it was her job to enforce it. It was my job to respect it even though I was a little disheartened and embarrassed standing there on the street with my unfinished hug hanging in the air between us.

If someone gets upset about your boundary, that's on them. It's not your job to process those feelings for them. It's only your job to take good care of you.

So if you're short on time, start with boundaries. Start saying no to demands on your time and energy.

Once the flow (or perhaps flood) of inbound requests cease, then we can take a look at what existing commitments we can take off our plates.

Simplification with the Eisenhower Matrix

In a business class, I was introduced to the idea of the Eisenhower Matrix. The 34th President of the United States, Dwight D. Eisenhower, created a way to organize his tasks based on urgency and importance. The four categories of his system include:

1. Urgent and important
2. Important but not urgent
3. Urgent and not important
4. Not urgent and not important

This system is meant to help you figure out what your priorities are, and then how you can slim down your list of to-dos to focus only on what matters. Here is the matrix:

	Urgent	Not Urgent
Important	Do it.	Schedule it.
Not Important	Delegate it.	Delete it.

We have to be as objective as possible when we are working with words like *urgent* and *important*. Always ask yourself if something is *really* urgent. Or is it *really* important? If there is a clear consequence of you not doing something, then it is probably important. If there is a clear consequence of you not doing something *now*, then it is probably urgent.

Once you've set your boundaries and are no longer adding things to your plate, sort your remaining tasks using this matrix.

Make a list. Put everything you do on this list. *Everything.*

Then start organizing and sorting your commitments into categories.

If it is urgent and important, and you are really the one who should do it, then keep doing it. Deadline-driven projects, taking care of yourself or someone else. Family emergencies.

If it is important but not urgent, then put it on the calendar. A lot of self-care could fit here. Exercise, cooking healthy meals, meditation sessions, journaling, hanging out with your friends.

If it is urgent but not important—and there are so many tasks that fall into this category—try to delegate as much of this as you can. These are all the little fires we run around trying to put out in a day. Interruptions like phone calls, emails, and messages. All those notifications that are always popping up and trying to steal our attention.

If it falls under the not urgent and not important category, this is your invitation to delete those tasks from your plate altogether. Wasting time on social media or screens (of which I am also guilty). Watching eight more episodes of your show in a single night.

But, Kory, you said you wanted me to prioritize joy! How can you say these things to me?

I do want you to prioritize joy. But joy and mindless consumption are not the same. If you are sacrificing your self-care time for mindless consumption, that needs to be addressed. Nothing wrong with being on social media or watching TV. I, for one, like to play video games. I'm currently working my way through all the endings of *Cyberpunk 2077*. I also spend a chunk of time on social media most days. But there needs to be moderation and balance in this and all things.

Trim down your to-dos, and get your time-wasting under control. Hopefully that will open up some room for you to add a bit of self-care. But let's assume you've slimmed down your schedule as much as you can without sacrificing your joy and you're still pressed for time.

Then let's look at the other self-care techniques you can do that require little to no time commitment on your part.

Breathe

Another catch your breath while running technique is literally breathing.

Learn how to pay attention to your breath. If you're rushing through the day, if you're feeling stressed. If you can register the tension in your shoulders or the sweaty palms—breathe.

Breathe.

Specifically, do box breathing.

Box breathing is when we imagine a square with its four sides. You inhale for four counts, hold for four counts, exhale for four counts, hold for four counts. Repeat.

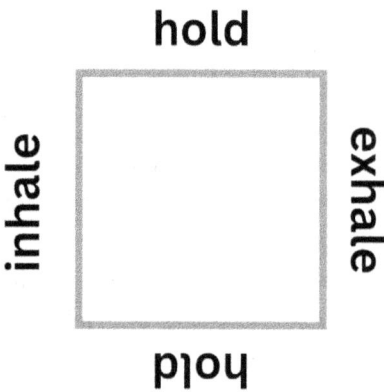

Box breathing is great for high-stress situations. I'd used box breathing in the past, but more recently, I use it before I go on stage. Like most people, I have a fear of public speaking. It doesn't matter that I know my message is important and that I want more than anything to help people. I still get scared. And when I get scared, my body thinks the best thing I could do at that moment is shit my pants.

This is not the best thing I can do in that, or any, moment. But especially not when I'm zipped into a one-piece jumper and mic'd up for all to hear.

So I breathe.

I breathe and quietly repeat this reminder to myself: *Ass tight, smile bright.*

Yes, I really say that.

But did you notice what I did there?

I brought friendliness to a scary moment. I do what I'd do for any friend who is scared and needs extra support. I'd try to make her laugh. Except the friend here is me.

This is what self-care, especially self-love, looks like while you're running. To be fully present with yourself.

Humor helps. Mantras help. But breathing helps more.

And there are so many ways to breathe! Ocean breath, belly breathing, lion's breath are some of my favorites—though some of these *will* draw a bit of attention. But there's also 4-7-8 breathing and diaphragmatic breathing.

The best part is that you can do breathing techniques anywhere, no extra time required. Hopefully you will already be breathing throughout the day. You need only bring a bit of attention to it.

Mindfulness

How do we become more aware in a world that is always vying for our attention?

Mindfulness.

Now, meditation is the mindfulness practice you've most likely heard of. But meditation is only one mindfulness practice. It may help to visualize the relationship between mindfulness and meditation like this:

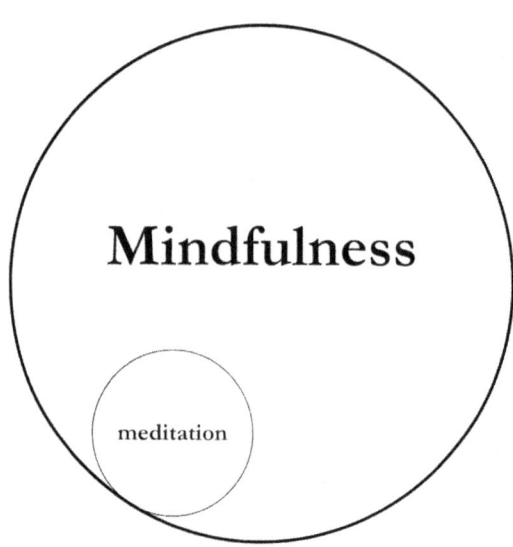

You can do nearly anything mindfully. It only requires that you start paying attention to yourself while you do the activity. To your actual movements, but also to your breath, to your moods, to your thoughts. Limiting multitasking and overstimulating yourself helps with this also. So does what I call peripheral focus.

Peripheral focus is when my attention is shifted more toward the periphery of my vision, or perhaps on my ears, than on what's dead center. My eyes are forward, slightly downward, but my attention is at each side. That's all mindfulness is: active attention.

Listening to your surroundings, tasting your food, whatever you do, do it mindfully.

And when you discover that your mind has wandered off, that you've started thinking about your to-do list or the bills, bring your attention back to the task at hand.

That's it. It's the commitment to coming back that's important. That's the part we want to get good at. It doesn't matter how many times you wander off. It matters only that you always come back to yourself.

If you do have a meditation practice, keep it up. If you don't and want one, you will find countless resources for how to meditate. And because there are so many different styles, I am sure you can find one that suits you. I share my three favorite meditation practices in a little e-book called **Your Wellness Blueprint.** You can read it for free by signing up for my newsletter at www.awellcaredforhuman.com.

The breathing exercise I mentioned earlier is also a mindfulness exercise. Many breathing techniques are. Again, none of this requires an extra time commitment. It only requires that you change how you're doing something in the moment.

But if you do have time to sit down and meditate for five, ten, or thirty minutes a day, fantastic.

If you don't, you can learn to catch your breath while rushing through your day.

Mental De-escalation

One of the most important skills I've learned on my mental health journey is de-escalation. This word may not mean anything to you, as it didn't mean anything to me either for a long time, so please allow me to paint a better picture.

Let's say that you had a long day at work. Let's also say that when you got home that night, tired, footsore, and later than you thought you would, you discover that the sink is full of dishes.

This visualization exercise works better if you are not the one who made the dishes. If the dishes were, in fact, made by a partner or child or roommate, and yet somehow here you are stuck with the responsibility of washing them.

Let's say that when you start washing them, you're only mildly annoyed that you're picking up someone else's slack. But by the time you've finished washing them, you're so mad, you're ready to burn down the house with the dishes and the people who made the dishes still inside.

How did you get this mad?

Because while you were washing the dishes, you were thinking, *No one appreciates me. No one cares how tired I am or how hard I work. After all I've done, they can't even be the smallest bit considerate of me?*

This is escalation. And we do this to ourselves all the time.

We escalate our pain and suffering by the stories we tell ourselves.

Housework is a good example for me because few things irritate me more than having to clean up someone else's mess. And my wife is the *messiest* person I know. I'm also currently in love with a dog that sheds a pound of hair a day. Hair doesn't weigh much. So a pound's worth is *a lot*.

For that reason, I've had significant practice with mental de-escalation.

But it isn't just with irritation that we escalate our emotions. Any emotion—fear and anxiety, sadness, depression, anger, sorrow, disappointment. We can build any emotion up to a fever pitch if we tell ourselves a good enough story and we sustain that story for long enough.

Here is what that looks like:

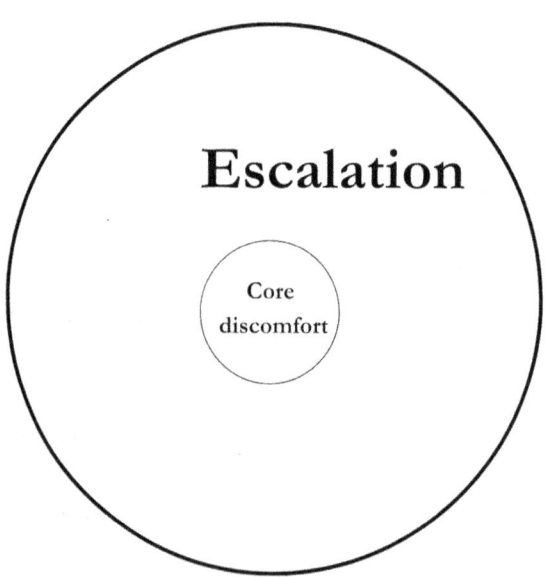

. . .

These are the two layers to most emotions. There is the initial discomfort of the situation, represented by the small circle. This could be the actual pain caused by a person or situation. We can call this the core discomfort. Then there is the way that the discomfort grows because of the stories we tell ourselves, represented by the larger circle depicting the expansion.

Another example of this is my medical anxiety. Because of a traumatic experience at the doctor when I was a child, going to see a doctor used to be incredibly difficult for me. I nearly had a panic attack each time. When they would take my blood pressure at the office during my appointments, it was always high. When I assured my doctor it was just *her* that was freaking me out, she asked me to buy an at-home pressure checker and send her the result. I did. A cool 107/65.

The reason I would get so scared at the office was because of the stories that my brain was telling me about all the horrible things that could happen to me there.

Fast forward to several years later with me having done significant de-escalation work.

I needed to give blood to get my cholesterol checked. I drove myself down to the lab, walked into the office, signed in, and waited for my name to be called. I was mildly nervous, but none of the cold-sweat, heart-pounding terror that I was used to when it came to medical stuff.

When they called my name, I went back into the little room and found two people instead of one.

And one of them looked young.

So young. Possibly sixteen years old.

"I'm training to be a phlebotomist!" she said, with all the zest and zeal that only a sweet soul who hasn't been crushed by the world yet can have. "I'll have my certificate by the time I graduate!"

From high school, certainly.

"How great for you," I said, wanting to be supportive. But inside I was thinking, *Oh my fucking*—and then, *Don't panic. Don't react. Let's work with this.*

But I was trying to be positive. I had enough awareness to know it was time to bring out the de-escalation tactics.

While I practiced de-escalation, the girl completed her prep work, got out her clean needle, and then inserted it. Only she couldn't find a vein.

I've always hated that. But this time I was breathing. I was smiling. I was trying to remain calm.

The supervising senior phlebotomist was issuing steady, clear instructions.

When she tried to reposition the needle as instructed, she pulled out too far and blood started pouring out of my open vein. The one she was essentially holding open with her poor needle placement.

The blood went *everywhere*.

Down my arm into the palm of my hand. All over my pants, the chair.

They were trying to get enough of my blood into the vial to make it count.

I was trying to breathe.

Finally, the girl got what she needed. The senior supervising phlebotomist handed me several wet wipes and the usual cotton ball/adhesive bandage combo for my elbow.

Then they were both looking at me, expecting me to freak out.

"I'm so sorry about that," the would-be phlebotomist said. She was clearly ready to get an earful.

Instead, I cried, "Good job! You were great! This is why we practice!"

I don't know if I was talking to her or talking to myself about de-escalation.

They blinked, probably waiting for me to realize my pants were soaked with blood.

I waved their concerns away. "It's *fine*. We're all ladies here. We know how to get blood out of clothes."

Laughs all around, though I couldn't tell if they were relieved or nervous laughs.

What they didn't know was that I wasn't upset because I was *so* proud of myself. I'd just had a major test to my medical anxiety and had passed. I felt amazing!

When I got back to my car, I texted everyone I had ever met and informed them of what an incredible breakthrough I'd just had. I sent everyone photos of my bloody arm and drenched clothes and recounted the story in full.

They bore this patiently until all that was left to do was to bask in my feelings of success, and to of course buy new jeans. Because the pair I had on were dead.

How did I practice de-escalation while blood was pouring out of my open vein? Breathwork, mindfulness, staying curious in the moment about what was going to happen. Time-traveling neither to the past to dwell on my terrible experiences, nor to the future, where I would assume that what came next would be worst.

I breathed. I asked questions.

Is this more or less painful than having a coyote rip off my arm? Certainly less. It's not that painful at all, just shocking to look at.

Is this what I thought would happen? Not at all. Then is it safe to assume I don't know what will happen next? Yes, very safe. Though I do hope the bleeding will stop. Then let's pay attention and see what it does...

That's it. I'm staying with myself and the experience. Nothing more, nothing less.

This practice of de-escalation can be used not just for irritation, anger, or anxiety. It can be used for any strong emotion that we are learning to build space around.

For a long time, you probably won't be entirely sure if you're getting better at de-escalation. It's possible you won't be able to see your progress until you encounter a challenging moment where your reaction is so different from your habitual response that you can't help but notice how far you've come.

Building space between emotional trigger and reaction happens in stages.

Stage zero: No awareness. In this stage you will do what you've always done (panic, scream, drink, etc.).

Stage one: Aware but habitual behavior continues. In this stage you can recognize you're upset, but you can't quite stop yourself from doing the habit.

Stage two: Aware but habitual behavior is intermittent. This stage is the same as one but you're more often successful at stopping yourself from doing the habit.

Stage three: Aware and there is no longer a habitual habit. At this point, when you are triggered, you can see that, feel your feelings, but you don't react in the habitual ways you did before.

Everything we learn to do for the mind—breathing, meditation, mindfulness—we are learning how to build the distance between trigger and reaction. Between feeling and behavior.

When I was bulimic, as soon as my craving was triggered, that was it. I'd go through the whole bulimic cycle very quickly. Or as is the case for my father, as soon as he was triggered, he would start screaming. That's what level zero looks like. There is little to no space between trigger and response. But with time, as our awareness and self-control increase, we can have very long pauses after our triggers. We can get so comfortable with them that we no longer react in those unhealthy ways.

Remember that the goal isn't to make the feelings go away. That's disrespecting our feelings.

Nor is the point to get good at pretending we don't have strong feelings. That's being dishonest with ourselves. We only need to work at de-escalation to the point that we are able to have whatever strong feeling we're having but it will not control our behavior.

Most of us go through life at stage zero, totally engrossed in the intensity of whatever we are experiencing, with little to no distance between ourselves and our emotions.

If you can elevate your awareness even just enough to notice that you're upset, you're already experiencing a shift and have moved to stage one. Stick with it. It doesn't mean you're a bad person if you're still out of control or that you'll never improve or never get ahold of yourself.

It takes time to address all the layers.

First there's the feeling and then there is your habitual behavior—the thing you always do when you feel this way.

For some of us the habitual behaviors are drinking, or smoking, or yelling, or binging, or crying.

There are as many habitual responses as there are people in the world. Part of the awareness is about you getting to know *your* habitual responses.

What do *you* do when you're scared? What do *you* do when you're upset?

We have to get good at building distance and slowing everything down. Noticing that you are doing the habitual behavior even if you aren't able to stop yourself quite yet is still a huge milestone. Don't undervalue that progress.

It can move so quickly. In one millisecond, we see something that pisses us off—dirty dishes—and in the next millisecond we're screaming at someone.

There is no distance there. No pause. No awareness.

We need to build those pauses and awareness into the moments in order to create the emotional distance we need to take back our self-control.

How do we do that?

We get so aware that we can feel the emotion rising up in us even if it's as fast as a cobra. We can feel it and dodge it before it strikes. Keep working on your meditation and mindfulness activities to develop this awareness.

You can also utilize the mindfulness check-in.

Throughout the day, check in with yourself. Whenever you think of it, do a body scan. Ask yourself how you're feeling. What sensations are present in your body? Take a look at your mind. What were you just thinking about?

Go ahead and check in with yourself right now. I'll wait.

Come on, do it. Even for sixty seconds.

This tactic of checking in, creating a pause, reminds me of a story I heard about Thich Nhat Hanh. If you've never heard of him, he was a Buddhist monk who lived in a monastery named Plum Village. In this monastery, they had a bell that would ring throughout the day. When the bell rang, everyone would stop what they were doing and listen.

I'm inviting you to do the same.

You don't have to have a bell. Maybe an alarm on your phone will do it. Or a calendar notification. You choose the trigger. But get in the habit of checking in with yourself. Of creating pauses.

You can do it as a listening meditation. I like this one because it's inconspicuous, which means I can do it anywhere, even in public places, and no one is going to know.

A listening meditation is where, like with the bell in Plum Village, you simply stop and listen to your surroundings for several moments. What do you hear?

Listen to what's close. Your own breath, maybe. Or the rustling clothes of someone who is sitting near you. Or perhaps the squeak of their shoes across tile. Now listen to something far away. Bird song, perhaps. A train whistling in the distance.

Many people think the point of meditation is to get really good at sitting in peacefulness no matter what might be going on in that head of yours. And sure, that's a useful skill.

But I think the more important skill is the ability to come back to ourselves.

There are five million distractions in a day. Another million reasons to get carried away by thoughts and feelings and our many to-dos. We have plenty of reasons to do anything and everything but check in. You could live your whole life that way.

Let's change that.

In addition to building this awareness and the ability to pay attention, which is what I was getting at with the bell exercise, it would also be useful to get used to treating your emotions as unruly children.

Emotions, like thoughts, can be befriended. I hope I made that clear already. The way to do that is to listen to them like a friend. Take in the information that they give you, but do not act on it. Pretend that your emotions have to fill out a form for every complaint they have.

Then put that form on a desk and say, "I will address this within three business days."

Building space between the event and your reaction to the event is very important.

Breathing is one way to lessen emotional reactivity. The listening exercise is another. The body scan is a third. The fourth is curiosity. Rather than assuming we know what will happen next, get curious to see what actually happens. Prepare to be surprised.

We can get very good at letting emotions roll over us like a wave without letting them control us and force us to act.

It comes down to practicing *not* reacting. You can redirect that energy by having an alternative action at the ready.

Maybe you tell yourself, "Every time I realize I'm getting pissed, I'm going to put on this birthday party hat. And while I wear it, I'm not allowed to do the habitual thing."

When you're mad enough to put a fist through a wall but you put on a birthday hat instead, it will seem ridiculous.

That's what makes it perfect. This unexpected action interrupts the strong emotion with its novelty and also interrupts the story you were telling yourself about it.

Instead of washing the dishes thinking about how no one loves you or cares about how tired and burned out you are, now you're washing dishes thinking, *What the fuck am I doing washing dishes in this cardboard party hat?*

Let go of the stories that feed strong emotions by bursting into song and dance. Michael Jackson's "Thriller," perhaps.

Doing something weird and perhaps a bit ridiculous like putting on a party hat while you're furiously scraping out an oatmeal bowl that *absolutely* should've been soaked—these are all de-escalation techniques. If you get numb to the weirdness of the party hat, pick your next weird thing. A clown nose, perhaps?

These are the good kinds of interruption.

Practice them.

Build space between you and the anger, or the sadness or fear, or whatever big feeling is coming up for you.

Again, the aim is not to rid ourselves of emotions. We don't want to do that anyway. We're trying to make friends with them. To be honest about what we're feeling, and to trust what we're feeling, and respect what we're feeling, and openly communicate what we're feeling.

Emotions are not a problem.

They're only worrisome when they force us to act in ways we don't want to—like yell, scream, throw things, or hurt ourselves or someone else. Or set our lives on fire.

Keep the feelings.

Lose the bad behavior.

And this is easiest to do if we aren't the ones fanning the flames.

When You Have a Little More Than No Time

Setting boundaries, simplifying your life, practicing mindfulness, mental de-escalation, and in-the-moment breathing techniques are impactful self-care techniques you can use with minimal time commitment. They are, as my friend Joe would say, learning to catch your breath while running.

But let's say you do have a little bit of time. Perhaps you started saying no and used the Eisenhower matrix with great success and now have more time for yourself, and are, wisely, looking to invest that extra time in your relationship with yourself. Where would your energy be best spent?

Let's say, for example, that you realize your relationship with your body is pretty good. And you think you have plenty of loving connections in your life too. But you struggle to connect with purpose, meaning, and joy (pillar three), and you feel like you struggle with strong emotions like anxiety and fear (pillar two).

With the little time you have, you could pick activities that focus on pillars two and three. Of course, keep doing whatever you're doing that has you enjoying a great relationship with your body and in your connections. But maybe you can also add mindfulness, meditation, mental de-escalation, therapy, or journaling to help you build a relationship with your mind & emotions. You can decide how much to commit to this—I suggest starting small.

Smaller.

No, even smaller than that.

So small that you think, *There's no way I can't not do that.*

Nothing derails me quicker than biting off more than I can chew and then getting discouraged that I can't make five thousand changes in the first hour of trying. If you choose meditation, make it five minutes of meditation, five minutes of journaling. If that feels too easy, move it up to seven or ten. That feels easy, move it up to fifteen, and so on.

Same for pillar three. Start asking yourself the right questions. What feels like play? When do you last remember having a good time? What did you do? Who was with you? What made it fun? What was something you've always wanted to do but you keep making excuses for—I don't have time, it's too expensive, I'll just embarrass myself anyway...

Then start small. Put something on the calendar *today*. But let it be a very doable something.

Let's pretend you always wanted to learn ice skating. A small step would be to find the local rink. The second small step would be to actually buy a pass for the day or make a date to go with a friend—nothing locks us in like accountability. Then once you show up at the place, do the next small thing. Put on the skates. The next small thing. Totter out to the ice. The next thing. Skate. The next thing. Fall down. The next thing. Get discouraged but don't give up because we're learning things—hurrah. Or so I tell myself. If you didn't love it like you thought you would, then don't push yourself. This is supposed to be joyful, after all.

You can also combine actions. Let's say you don't have a ton of time for self-care, but you feel like all of your pillars need *something*. Then find an activity that will help you build all the pillars at once.

Let's say you choose a yoga class. Yoga will help you build a relationship with your body. It will teach you mindfulness. It can be joyful. And if you do the yoga in an actual class, you can make friends and connections or at least put yourself out there to do so. That's one activity for all four pillars.

Or if you like sports.

Perhaps you live near a community center that has adult intramural leagues. You sign up for flag football and join an open team. You get exercise (body pillar), you're having fun (spirit pillar), you're making friends with all those sweaty people you're running around with (connection pillar). And depending on how competitive you are as a person, you'll have plenty of opportunity to work with your big feelings on the field (mind & emotions pillar).

My point here is that you can do this. With little to no time, you can do this. Step by step, shift your life with small, incremental changes. Even if you're exhausted, even if you're overworked and burned out, even if you have no hope that anything will change.

Do it anyway.

What have you got to lose?

What do you stand to gain?

Key Chapter Takeaways

- When we don't have much time for self-care, we can focus our efforts on tactics that require little to no time but will yield high results such as setting boundaries, time management strategies, breathing techniques, mindfulness, and mental de-escalation.
- When we do have time, add in relationship-building activities from any or all of the pillars as time allows.
- Choose self-care techniques that target multiple pillars at once, as a way to save on time.
- If we can do only one thing for ourselves, let it be building awareness. Awareness is the basis of all personal transformation. We can't correct a problem we don't see. And we can't see it if we don't have awareness.

PILLAR BREAKERS

Another way to practice self-care that requires little to no time commitment is by addressing pillar breakers. There are certain things that we do that destroy our pillars. This is unfortunate because no one wants to hear that while they are working hard to build up their relationship with themselves, they might also be the one making it worse. I call these bad habits pillar breakers, and these pillar breakers are what undo all of our hard work.

What breaks our pillars:

1. Negative thoughts and speech
2. The FOG
3. Shame
4. Using self-care as self-punishment
5. False narratives

Why does it matter, knowing about the pillar breakers?

Because self-care isn't only what we do *for* ourselves, it's also what we *stop* doing *to* ourselves.

What is it we can stop doing?

Criticizing ourselves, judging ourselves, being too hard on ourselves, expecting too much of ourselves, doing things out of obligation when we know we should say no, doing things out of guilt when we know we should say no. Doing things out of fear when we know we should say no. Doubting ourselves, not trusting ourselves, talking poorly about our ourselves, in our head or aloud to others.

For many years, it was true that the people hurting me most in life were my family. It is also true that after I removed myself from the situation, the person who hurt me the most was *me*.

I don't love that. But it's true.

The same can be said of my mother.

Her family did terrible—truly evil—things to her. They hurt her and betrayed her in countless ways. But she also hurt and betrayed herself.

Breaking the cycle meant that I had to be the one to stop hurting myself.

I want to use the metaphor of a venomous snake. I also want to make a disclaimer here that I actually love snakes. They are a vital and important part of our ecosystems, and frankly, they're cool. It's not fair they get a bad rap. But I also want to lean into that stereotype a little here for illustrative purposes, so forgive me, my dear serpents.

Let us say that you are in the presence of a venomous snake. This snake bites you. Now, obviously, you have a problem.

The first step would not be to have a good think about why that snake might have bitten you. Reflection is a useful healing tool, but it has its time and place. Your actual first step would be to get away from the snake. (I don't want you to kill it. It's not its fault that it felt threatened and defended itself. Also, I told you I like them).

The appropriate response is to get away from the snake so that it can't bite you again.

If you are in the vicinity of venomous snakes who have bitten you, please get away from them. Get safe first.

Once you do, you still need to address the venom that's currently coursing through your veins.

It didn't go away just because the snake is gone.

It wasn't enough for me to get away from my family of biters.

When I left, I carried the negative effects of all that trauma, the venom, around with me for years. The symptoms of that venom included fears, limiting self-beliefs, survival mechanisms, poor coping skills, a warped view of myself cultivated by manipulation and gaslighting.

The same may be true for you.

I want to say something here about trauma. Often people—myself included—tend to measure trauma in quantities. I've been guilty of saying, "Yeah, these things happened, but it's not as bad as what *he* went through."

You may not have been exposed to an entire family of venom-spitters, but that doesn't mean that you should minimize the effects of what you were exposed to. Venom is still dangerous, in any quantity. So even if your experiences are not as extreme as someone else's, that doesn't mean you should disregard your own suffering.

The good news is that the techniques I recommend in this chapter apply to all venom, no matter how much or how little you've got.

But I will always suggest that the most important first move is to get somewhere safe. Get away from the snakes.

Once you've done that, or if you've at least put some boundaries in to minimize the risk of being bitten again, then let's look at common types of venom that might be in your system, and what sort of antivenom you can use to neutralize its effects.

Pillar Breaker: Negativity

I've heard Buddhist gurus give lengthy speeches about how there is no such thing as a positive event or a negative event. That all events are only events. We are the ones who imbue those experiences with meaning. That sounds beautiful and may be true, but I am not so enlightened. When I say something is negative, I am pointing out its ability to bring me down, to upset me, destabilize me, or straight up ruin my day.

Protecting ourselves from negative thoughts and speech is one of the critical self-care practices that fall under the "Things We Should Stop Doing" header.

If you, like me, have a habit of criticizing yourself, giving yourself a hard time, thinking poorly of yourself, know that this is a habit you can break.

This judgmental and cruel inner voice likely came from a snake. In my case, from my father mostly, but also other villains who crossed the stage of my life briefly on their cues.

Before I share how to rid yourself of this venomous negativity, I just want to say that if someone speaks terribly to you, they don't deserve access to you. Your company is a privilege. Some people do not deserve that privilege.

This holds true even if that someone is a parent who was supposed to have lifetime access to you. If they've violated the unspoken contract of kindness, they have lost the right to that privilege. They're adults. They know there are consequences to their actions. Don't feel like you're doing them some great injustice. They had a job to love you unconditionally and they did not do it. The end.

It need not be any more complicated than that.

If, however, you've decided to keep the person(s) in your life, and there are many good reasons to do this, what are you going to do to protect yourself from their negativity?

Avoid certain topics? Limit your time and exposure to this person? Always meet on neutral ground like a coffee shop or restaurant, anywhere you know they will be on their best behavior because there are too many eyes on them?

Remember this is only to protect yourself from additional bites and venomous injections—which will keep you unwell. Do whatever you have to do to limit the chances they will bite you again. Do not give them the opportunity if you can help it.

As for the venom already in your veins, we must address that separately.

There are many ways negativity can present itself in the mind.

Perhaps you have a cruel voice that always tells you that you're not good enough, points out all the things that are wrong with you, how you'll never measure up.

Perhaps you always expect the worst possible outcome of any situation, because it was your experience that the worst *did* happen. Repeatedly and often.

Perhaps you're reluctant to even get your hopes up because they were crushed in the past and you refuse to go through that again.

These are only three examples of negativity venom.

In all cases, our ability to transmute negativity venom will require a certain level of awareness. As mentioned, you can't fix what you can't see.

Awareness and mindfulness, and also gentle redirection, are the antivenom to negativity. As you use mindfulness to develop your awareness, you will find it easier to catch yourself being negative.

I have a new dog. We adopted Max from the humane society. He's the cutest dog in the world, in my opinion. If you don't think so, you're wrong. Sorry.

When Max came to us, he had a few habits from his old life as a stray that I wanted to break.

His tendency to take my entire hand into his mouth when he wanted affection, for example.

Every time he did it, I had to remind him with a gentle "no," then give him a toy to redirect that chewing energy. This showed him what was appropriate to chew since my flesh was not an option.

In a few short weeks, he has stopped chewing on my hand. I'm very happy about that.

Your mind, through repeated exposure to negativity, has picked up the habit of negativity.

This is not your fault. You were reacting to your environment and your circumstances.

However, negativity is not a habit one should live with all their lives.

You can retrain your mind out of its bad habits like the cutest, smartest dog in the world. I do not mean this to be condescending. I'm not saying you're only as smart as a dog.

But our minds are built for learning and efficiency, and it achieves that efficiency by turning as many actions as it can into habits we can perform instantly. This is not so great when the habits are unhealthy ones.

Interrupt the bad behavior—being negative—and correct that behavior with a more suitable one. What the more suitable behavior will be is up to you, as you have many options and only you can decide what kind of person you want to grow into.

It may help to fill in this blank: Every time _____ happens, I wish I was the kind of person who _____.

I will say that obviously we can't address negative thoughts and negative speech with more negativity. Telling myself, *Stop being so mean to yourself, you idiot! You're awful!* never got me anywhere.

Pillar Breaker: The FOG

In this context, FOG stands for fear, obligation, and guilt. This acronym was first coined by Susan Forward and Donna Frazier in their book *Emotional Blackmail*. It refers to how toxic or narcissistic parents will use fear, obligation, and guilt to control their children's behaviors. I don't think you need to have a toxic parent, however, to have encountered feelings of fear, obligation, and guilt. Any abusive or toxic person or situation will also use FOG.

Many of us have experienced the pressure to deprioritize our own needs for the sake of someone else's, and at the center of that pressure, what drives it, builds it, and sustains it, is often fear, obligation, or guilt.

Take the story I told you at the beginning of this book, when my mother suffered her brain injury from my uncle's assault. Every decision and move I made in the following weeks were made out of fear, obligation, and guilt.

I was afraid that if I didn't protect her, the worst would happen. I felt obligated to protect her because she was my mother. And I felt guilty for not doing more for her—even though I didn't have the resources to do more—because it felt like she was my responsibility. I'm sure there was also guilt that I had not done more to protect her from him, though that was also not my responsibility.

Fear, obligation, and guilt are all venom. When we are deep in the FOG, we cannot see ourselves, our responsibilities, or our lives clearly. We often act from an instinctual place, an unhealed place, rather than for our highest good.

But doing something out of fear, a sense of obligation, or guilt is never in our best interest.

We neutralize these venoms the same way we neutralize other venoms.

We can use mindfulness and shadow work practices to get to know our fears, sense of obligation, and guilt. Raising awareness around when these feelings come up and why they come up will weaken their hold on us. Then we can practice resisting our "bad" habits—our poor coping skills, codependency, reactivity, submission—whatever habits you currently have in place that arise when confronted with the FOG.

A note here: fear, obligation, and guilt are all strong emotions.

It can be difficult to redirect the energy of a strong emotion when we are caught up in the moment. If you develop enough awareness to realize that your fear is in control and that you reacted poorly, rather than in the way you wanted to, try not to beat yourself up about this. You're still making progress.

I don't need to tell you that there are plenty of people out there reacting in the FOG with no self-awareness at all. Give yourself a break if you fail to live up to your high expectations. You want to always, above all, react to yourself as a good friend would. This is part of having a great relationship with yourself. The ability to still talk to yourself with love and compassion when you make mistakes is a core attribute of that self-love.

Don't give up on yourself too soon.

Pillar Breaker: Shame

Brené Brown's earlier TedTalk is an amazing primer on shame. If you haven't watched it, I highly encourage you to. In fact, I recommend all of her work in this area. She can tell you far more about it than I can.

What I can say is that shame is a complex emotional response.

Shame tells us, "I am bad. I am a mistake." It's the "I am" part, that focus on the self, that lets you know that what you are working with is shame rather than guilt. Guilt focuses on behavior. "I did this and that was the wrong thing to do."

The problem with shame is that it can be a big blockage to loving ourselves. If we are ashamed of who we are, if we feel like there is something fundamentally wrong with us, it can be hard to feel love toward ourselves. Shame will always make us feel like we are worthless, bad, and a blight on this world. That we are a burden. We're too much. We're a problem.

And it's hard to love yourself if you're convinced that you're not worth loving because there is something wrong with you.

In my own life, my shame was at its peak when I was in my early twenties. My father's narcissistic abuse and constant criticism had created a core belief that I was lacking and unworthy. I'd heard this criticism so much that his voice had become a permanent resident in my mind.

But I developed shame from other negative experiences as well.

When I'd been outed and then ruthlessly bullied for it in high school. That also made me ashamed of who I was.

Every time a partner cheated on me, I felt ashamed. Like perhaps the reason for their bad behavior was that I wasn't enough to keep a person happy.

When my grandfather slapped me across the face and called me a liar even though I'd told the truth, I felt shame. Indignation, but also shame.

Every time I felt less worthy because my clothes came from the Salvation Army or that I lived in a trailer with my mom rather than a nice house like some of my friends. Whenever my physical imperfections were pointed out or ridiculed—all of this together compounded my shame.

It's possible that there may be not just one experience that convinced you that you're "bad," but a chorus of voices, events, and experiences that have accumulated and compounded over the course of your life.

Shame can also be hard to recognize because it's a difficult feeling we usually try to avoid. I've yet to meet anyone who can look directly at their shame with ease. Even the bravest of us flinch when we try.

Looking at shame may seem terrifying, but it is the first step toward pulling its fangs out of the back of your neck.

The biggest reason to process and transmute this venom called shame is because as long as it is poisoning our system, it will feel impossible to love ourselves.

One thing I can tell you with confidence is that there is no amount of shame that you can't transform. When my shame was at its peak, when I was at my loneliest, most self-loathing, most suicidal, most bulimic, most depressed, most anxious, most poor, and most addicted, I was still able to do this work.

My experiences align with Brené Brown's research about shame. In her talk, she says that shame is highly correlated to addiction, depression, aggression, violence, eating disorders, bullying, and suicide. That these are manifestations of shame.

I can attest to that.

Can you ever be completely free of your shame?

I don't know.

Mine still surprises me sometimes. It rears up in unexpected moments, but it no longer controls my behavior like it used to. It no longer adds gloom to my days or makes it hard to breathe or exist. It can still show up for dinner on occasion, which in all honesty, I don't particularly *enjoy*.

But the visits are rare and what we're striving for is progress, not perfection.

We may not be able to banish shame from our lives completely, since it seems to be part of the human emotional toolbox. However, we can develop such a tolerance to it that it is no longer capable of debilitating us.

I am no longer in danger of dying from shame, and that feels like a tremendous win to me. Shame is one of the most dangerous venoms for this reason—for its high correlation to suicide.

That's why it's so important to address it. That starts with having the courage to look at it.

And after we gain the courage to start looking at our shame, take its measure, where do we go from there?

We can avoid the things that make shame more powerful and do the things that diminish it.

What makes shame more powerful? Secrecy, hiding ourselves away, being silent about what's happened to us or the way people have hurt us, judging ourselves harshly. All of that breeds shame.

It wasn't until I started working with a therapist and finally started talking about some of the things that had happened to me that I began to see myself and my situation differently.

When we keep all the venom inside, we don't always see things clearly. It's much easier to get confused and blame yourself when you keep it inside. When we get it out, when we share it with trusted others, they can point out how, in fact, you're not as to blame as you think.

This begins to open our mind to other possible storylines.

Shame is also diminished in the presence of empathy. In practicing self-compassion for ourselves, we come to know that we're *not* the only one who experiences shame from mistreatment or rejection. Or we're not the only human in history to make a huge mistake and feel bad about it.

Not even close.

Everyone is good at hiding their shame. Everyone is good at not talking about it. But everyone *does* experience shame. At the end of her talk, Brown says that the most powerful thing we can do when we see someone struggling with shame is to reach out and say, "Me too."

This is because shame creates a feeling of exclusion. That we are set apart from others by our wrongness.

Connection dispels that sense of isolation and brings us back into the circle, reminding us that we aren't so different from everyone else. That even our darkest secrets and worst mistakes on the planet are being shared by other people too.

Because we're human.

We're just human.

But you can't process that shame and dispel the myth of isolation unless you open up to someone and reestablish that connection with others.

So if you are struggling with shame, invest in connection. Share your dark thoughts with a professional or a trusted friend.

Whatever you do, don't play pretend.

Don't keep this venom in.

If you do, the risk of it killing you is high.

Self-Care as Self-Punishment

Let me tell you about the time I had my eyebrow shaved off in the Philippines.

My wife's baby brother was getting married, and she and I were part of the wedding party. As anyone who has ever been part of a wedding party knows, you're expected to get done up before the wedding. It doesn't matter that I always look like a two-timing aunty from a telenovela whenever I get my hair done in the Philippines, I understood what was expected of me.

We reported to the correct hotel room at the correct time for the preparations.

When it was my turn in the hair and makeup chair, the makeup artist pulled out a razor blade.

I froze.

"Um, excuse me. What is that for?" I pointed at the razor blade

"To shave your eyebrows," he said in his thick Filipino accent. His tone implied that I was an idiot.

First of all, I don't grow eyebrows. There's nothing to shave. As I mentioned, I overplucked my brows in the nineties to mimic the style of pop stars like Christina Aguilera and Gwen Stefani. What I didn't know at the time is that if you do this enough, it damages the hair follicle and they will never grow back.

My eyebrows are now naturally thin forever more. Whenever I try to grow them out, I get nothing more than a few stray hairs near my eyelid.

So imagine my confusion when this man expressed a desire to shave my brows.

I looked to my sister-in-law, who was in the chair beside me, as my wife was nowhere to be found.

"It's just how we do it here," she said. "Tweezing is sort of an American thing."

She would know. Both she and my wife had lived in the Philippines until they immigrated to America for their graduate degrees.

"Okay," I said, though I was pretty sure there was nothing for this man to shave off.

But I didn't want to make a fuss.

I didn't want to be a bother.

So what did I do?

I let the man *shave my face*. With a razor blade.

Once the makeup and hair were done, I inspected my face for signs of damage, but it was fine. I still looked like a telenovela aunty, there was no way around that. But at least it looked like I had eyebrows.

It wasn't until after the wedding when my wife and I had gone back to our hotel room at the end of the long and exhausting day that I discovered the truth.

Because when I washed off all that thick telenovela makeup, I also washed off one of my eyebrows.

Just one.

After I got over the shock of the fact that this man had hidden his crime under makeup, I immediately started beating myself up about it:

Oh god, I knew I should've told him no. Why do I let people talk me into things I don't want to do! How stupid do I have to be to let a stranger shave my face!

Quickly, this internal rage spilled out, and my wife was forced to listen to my rant while trying not to laugh about my brow.

This is often how we speak to ourselves.

Not just when we go against our better judgment and blame ourselves for our own perceived stupidity, but also when we take care of ourselves.

We diet because we hate the way our body looks. We exercise because we want to be a different size or shape.

We do self-care, even self-care that properly targets the four pillars, from a place of self-loathing. We do it because there's something wrong with us that needs to be fixed.

But as long as we view ourselves as something wrong that needs to be fixed—whether that wrongness is our body or personality or interests or income or singleness, whatever—the self-care won't amount to anything.

I call this self-care as self-punishment.

Self-care as self-punishment never yields the benefits of self-care. We will never feel cared for if the person who is supposed to love us (in this case, ourselves) is always pointing out everything that is wrong with us, everything that is bad, and everything that needs to be fixed, and all the ways we don't measure up.

How we speak to ourselves as we perform self-care tasks matters. How we think of ourselves as we perform self-care matters too.

All of the venomous, habitual pillar breakers I introduced in this chapter—negativity, the FOG, and shame—drive us to practice self-care as self-punishment.

If we want our self-care to amount to anything, if we want the benefits of self-care to actually heal us and transform our lives, we have to make sure that our self-care isn't self-punishment.

We will never have a strong and healthy relationship with ourselves until we do.

Shadow Work: The Work of Transmutation

How do we befriend those pesky inner demons?

Shadow work.

What is shadow work?

The term *shadow work* is often used in two different contexts: in a psychological context and a spiritual context.

In the psychological context, we get the term *shadow* from Carl Jung. Jung was a Swiss psychologist and psychiatrist.

If you've ever heard of introverted and extroverted personality types, archetypes, the collective unconscious—then you've heard about Jung's work.

According to Jung, the shadow is our unknown dark side. The shadow includes all the pieces of our personalities that we've repressed or rejected for one reason or another.

How much we've repressed or rejected will determine how much power our shadows have over our lives. The more awareness we have, the less of our psyche will dwell unseen in the shadow.

Jung didn't view our shadow as evil or as a malevolent force, nor do I.

In fact, Jung argues that many positive traits can be uncovered when connecting with our shadow and by working with the shadow to integrate its wisdom. If we do that, we can strengthen its positive qualities while weakening or balancing the negative aspects like negative thoughts and speech.

There are some people who believe that your shadow—your karma—could have begun its development ten, twenty, or a hundred lifetimes ago and the condition that your shadow is in now and how well you resolve its issues carries over from lifetime to lifetime.

An absolutely depressing idea if you ask me.

The last thing I want to find out is that I've been an anxious nutcase for centuries. Possibly millennia.

Regardless of what you believe, I am one hundred percent certain you've met unhealed people who have not befriended their dark side. Hurt people hurt people. And I don't know about you, but I'm trying to be the kind of person who doesn't hurt others, which means I need to keep an eye on my shadow.

A lot of my personal shadow work involves working with my fears. Fear is a core aspect of my shadow. Some people have a lot of self-loathing in their shadows which makes it hard to befriend the darkness. It's equally difficult if the shadow is full of shame.

The qualities of your shadow will be unique to you, based on the experiences that created it. If you struggle with strong emotions like anger, jealousy, loneliness, cynicism, hopelessness, or fear, that's your shadow. Arrogance, helplessness, addiction, depression, anxiety, if you're quick to judge—you'll find these in your shadow too.

Speaking of judgment, don't give yourself a hard time about having any or all of these traits. We all have traits we aren't proud of. Accepting this fact is a great first step toward befriending them.

I can be very envious, for example. Growing up, it was hard to feel grateful when it felt like all the other kids had better families, better lives, better opportunities.

Even though I have healed a lot and found a lot of peace, I sometimes still hear a little voice that says, *But what about me?*

That's little Kory who was abused and neglected. She lives in my shadow. I am as responsible for her as I am all the other parts of my well-being. And because it's important, I'll say it again: having a shadow isn't bad. We just need to be aware of ours and manage them accordingly.

When my shadow remained unseen, when I never shined light on it, when I never acknowledged its presence or voice, when I criticized myself rather than embraced this as part of my human experience, my fears got bigger because I was continuing to inflict the damage upon myself that others had inflicted.

If we're too scared to look, and many of us are, the shadow will remain quite powerful.

If the shadow is strong, then our fears and inner critics are quite loud.

If I don't keep an eye on my shadow or notice when it walks through the door, my fear is going to run me around. It will make decisions for me, it will lash out at people I love. It will have me feeling anxious about my future, and jealous of my friends, and worried about my perceived failures.

The shadow might keep me from doing the things I want to do or from forming healthy connections I want to form because I'm too scared to do so.

The tools for addressing the unhealed shadow are the same as other healing tools we've explored: developing awareness so we can see when the negativity is poisoning us. Then redirecting the negativity, disrupting its habitualness by replacing it with a more useful habit.

If you have the habit of always speaking unkindly to yourself, what can you say to yourself instead? (If you have no idea, consider what you've always wished your abuser or bully would have said to you.)

If you have a habit of always complaining about yourself to others, how else might you talk about yourself? Might I recommend making a list of things you appreciate about yourself?

When strong emotions come up, it's important to interrupt them so they don't escalate. But you get to choose what this redirection looks like.

You can create the habit of always psyching yourself up when you get scared.

You can develop the habit of always using humor when anxiety shows up.

You can hone the habit of bravery in the face of your biggest fears. Maybe each time you get scared, you vow to proudly declare, "Time to put on my bow tie of bravery!"

When you find yourself feeling envious and left out, perhaps you can reinforce the habit of counting your blessings and believing that not all that shines is gold. Sometimes what is a blessing for others wouldn't be the least bit good for you.

It's important to believe that we aren't stuck with our bad habits forever.

If you learned it, you can unlearn it. I know this to be true because I have unlearned more things than some people have learned in a lifetime.

Don't fear your shadow and what you find there.

The shadow can teach us a lot about ourselves. It can help us to understand ourselves, our experiences, and point out where we keep getting stuck. Shadow wisdom shows us where we are holding ourselves back and teaches us how to set ourselves free.

Emotional triggers are often my cue that an unhealed wound is present.

Strong reactions often come from the shadow.

Instead of feeling bad about the way you reacted to something, ask yourself, "What did my shadow just reveal to me? What was that about?"

Apart from looking at emotional triggers, another way to glimpse your shadow is to look at the patterns playing out in your life.

Is there something you keep doing? Is there a certain kind of experience that keeps happening to you over and over again? If there is a cycle that replays itself over and over, if you have an unhealthy dating pattern, for example, chances are your shadow is driving you into a certain situation over and over again in order to teach you something vital.

My early romantic relationships followed a pattern. First, I would become completely infatuated with someone. Then I would try to rescue them from themselves. Of course this didn't work. We would be together for a while and they would get very cozy with how nurturing I was, then they would take that for granted and cheat on me. And then we'd break up but only so that I could find someone else to do this with again.

That pattern didn't stop until I did the shadow work to process my codependency and address my abandonment and attachment issues.

Where in your life do you have a repeating cycle that you'd like to change? Look closer at that. It could be around anything—relationships, money, living situations, jobs, addictions—anything.

But start looking. The shadow is tricksy. She likes moving unseen. If she realizes you're searching for her, she'll slink away if she can.

Don't give up if you can't spot her right away. Just pretend you're playing hide and seek with a cat and that the more you figure out her hiding places, the more you'll understand her.

Going back into your childhood is definitely worth a look, if you can stand it. It might help to write down your worst memories, not just to get them out of your head and put them to rest but so that you can reread them to yourself and see if you can spot any patterns. Again, I recommend a professional if you have some dark stuff to work through.

In addition to reviewing your past experiences, you could try this writing prompt:

"As a child, it was always expected that I would…"

Now answer what it was your caregivers expected from you. Or teachers. Or friends. Or family. Anyone who comes to mind.

For me, as a child I was always expected to be emotionless.

My father was always telling me not to cry.

"Kory, you're too emotional. If you don't get that under control, you're going to be just like your crazy mother."

You can also say to yourself, "I felt judged when..." and explore those moments when others tried to make you feel bad about who you really are.

Feeling judged is really hurtful. It's possible that we tucked pieces of ourselves away into our shadows in order to avoid letting others see the parts they rejected. One awful (and usually jealous) person said one awful (and usually jealous) thing and now we're hiding our gifts away so that no one else will be mean to us about them.

It might also help to make a list of your fears. I'm afraid of being eaten alive by a crocodile, poverty, losing my teeth, dark, deep water I can't see into—probably because of the crocodiles.

It doesn't help that I am inconveniently prey-sized, which is unfortunate. And I've seen a horrifying video where an enormous Nile crocodile leapt out of the water and ate a whole cheetah.

No thank you.

But I'm also scared of making a fool of myself in front of others, public humiliation of any kind—wait, why did I say it would be helpful to make a list of your fears? I'm terrified just thinking about all of this.

Ah, right. A list like this is ripe for shadow work.

Look at your own fears and figure out if there are any hidden, repressed traits in there that you can look at more closely and bring to light.

The goal of shadow work is integration. Writing and producing the *Who Killed My Mother?* podcast was, at its heart, a shadow work project. And what I got out of it by doing it was a lot of integration. A better understanding of what happened to my mother, our relationship and our family dynamics, how it all fit together.

Being able to process everything removed all the hurt that had been left between us, and that's essentially what you're aiming for here as well with your own shadow work.

That's why it can be hard to do shadow work. There was probably a reason why you repressed or rejected these pieces of yourself, and to go back and look at that pain doesn't feel *awesome*. But I would say—and this is just my opinion—that it's worth it because of the peace and strength you can gain from that integration.

I don't know about you, but when I'm hurt and exhausted, I'm willing to do just about anything for peace and strength.

Shadow work could be the release you're looking for.

But the goal in this shadow exploration is not to retraumatize yourself. You don't need to process thirty years of trauma in a weekend of contemplation or a few journaling sessions.

Give yourself five to ten minutes a day, in the morning, at night, during lunch, whenever you have those five minutes, and write about those patterns you see, the pillar breakers you're using and how you'd like to change them, review and rewrite painful memories you have, or try out the prompts I suggested. Look at any shame you have, asking yourself to make a log of all the times, places, events, and people who made you feel like there was something wrong with you, that you were bad, that you were not enough.

Whatever you're drawn to, start there.

I say five to ten minutes because you don't need a ton of time for this. You want to take shadow work slowly. You don't need to have long (and exhausting) journaling sessions about your past hurts in order to create big shifts.

But I do invite you to do some exploration. We can usually learn a lot about ourselves by examining the type of venom(s) we have coursing through our proverbial veins.

Key Chapter Takeaways

- Self-care isn't just what we do *for* ourselves, it's also what we *stop* doing *to* ourselves.
- It is one thing to escape an abuser or a toxic situation. It is another to heal the effects of those experiences.
- Pillar breakers such as negativity, shame, self-punishment, and the FOG are habitual responses that will destroy our relationship with ourselves and diminish any good effects

from self-care. We must break these habits as soon as we can.
- Better habits such as awareness, curiosity, redirection, and self-compassion can be done in the course of a day, and do not require an additional time commitment, only an emotional commitment to practice them as the opportunities to do so arise.
- Shadow work can create big shifts in how we see ourselves and our experiences, and for that reason, may be worth exploring.

FALSE NARRATIVES

Sometimes the biggest lie we tell is the lie we tell ourselves, or at least, they are certainly the most convincing lies. Or there are times when people we love, people we trust, write these false stories about us. And we believe these false narratives with our whole heart because we want to believe the people we love. Their stories of us become our stories.

If these stories are untrue, then they can do a lot of damage to our relationship with ourselves and wreak a lot of havoc on our lives.

I have clear moments in my life when I, with awareness, saw false narratives for what they were and was able to set myself free of them. It's this clarity that often causes the initial shift away from a false narrative.

Imagine you'd heard a rumor several times. Each time the rumor gets back to you, it's a little different, until you really start to question if it's real at all.

The transformation of false narratives begins with awareness, but equally useful is curiosity. Just like a rumor, if you were to get curious about whether or not the story was actually true, you're already gaining the upper hand. Just by questioning it, you've disempowered it a bit.

Not only will curiosity stop us from forming new false narratives, but it will help us to dissolve current false narratives. When your developing awareness alerts you to the possibility that you've got a false narrative running in your head, get curious.

Is this story about me really true? Is it even my story at all? Or did someone assign this story to me? Remember that honesty and open communication are parts of a good relationship with yourself. Be honest now.

I've used this technique of getting curious with much success. Just this leaning in, rather than pulling away, is enough to start dissolving it. Dissolving false narratives isn't so different than shadow work.

Shadow work is meant to help us see the full picture, the truth.

Dispelling false narratives does the same.

There are gifts and talents hidden in your shadow. When you splintered yourself and hid parts of yourself away to survive whatever you've survived, you locked those gifts and talents away. Same for false narratives. My father used to treat my imagination like a big problem, and it made me shy away from using it.

He said, "Get your head out of your ass. We're living in the real world."

But my imagination is one of my greatest strengths.

Get curious about what you've got hidden in the stories you've heard about yourself. Don't expect just to find dark and terrible things. Expect to find magic and power.

It is true that getting to know yourself is hard because it's like getting to know the school pariah. You're intrigued, but there are a lot of rumors about her. Everyone has an idea of who she is and what she's done. You're trying to see past that to the truth that lies beneath. It's tricky business.

But in this business of building a strong relationship with yourself, that's exactly what's happening. You're pursuing self-discovery in spite of the rumors and narratives.

Do you know who you are despite all the stories that people tell about you? And that even *you* tell about yourself?

Your friends, your family, and even strangers who have spared little more than a passing glance in your direction, they all think they've got a good idea of who you are. We can't do much about the stories that other people make up about us, I'm afraid.

But we can focus on looking at, dissecting, and releasing the stories we have about ourselves.

It's these stories we tell ourselves about ourselves that are the problem.

These stories generate fear. They limit us. They make the world a very small and difficult place to live in.

Just like the rumors, false narratives aren't all that accurate.

Who Killed My Mother? is about my discovery of a pretty big false narrative. I had a whole story about my mother and me, our relationship, what it was and wasn't. What those experiences meant and didn't. Her death and all that happened after caused a pretty big shift for me that essentially laid those false narratives to rest. I didn't see myself or her, or the life we shared, the same way once the truth came out.

Another moment of transformational insight was when I learned the truth about my father's crime.

It was never a secret that he'd gone to prison. My mother had even brought me to the penitentiary to visit him. "And to beg for money," he'd added later.

When I was older, I asked my father about his crime. I knew he'd been forced to register as a sex offender for a number of years, but I wasn't really clear on what he'd done.

The story he painted was one of dubious consent. Like perhaps the woman had changed her mind during intercourse but it was only her word against his. That it wasn't—in his opinion—really an offense and that he wouldn't have even gone to trial at all if not for my mother. He made it seem that my mother had lied about him, and that she was to blame for his incarceration.

I remember sitting in the court room with my grandmother at the ruling. I remember the surprised look on my father's face when they sentenced him to sixteen years, though he would only serve about three and a half. I didn't understand what was happening, as it was only two days after my fifth birthday. Because I had no clear memories beyond these fragments, I accepted my father's story as an honest one.

Not long ago I found a newspaper article from that week in August

1988, the week he'd been convicted. The front page of that week's edition had been scanned and preserved online, and to my surprise, there was an article outlining the details of my father's crime at the bottom of that first page.

This article says my father went up to a woman's door, knocked on it, and asked for sugar. That he then put a knife to her throat and forced her to the bedroom, where he assaulted her. That the assistant DA dropped the first-degree rape and sexual offense charges in exchange for my father pleading guilty to second-degree rape and sexual offense.

This was about as far from my father's story in both content and tone as I could imagine, so learning the true nature of his crime was rather shocking.

In my mind, it is a very different person who could commit an act like this. It is far more malicious to stalk a woman long enough to know that she is home alone, far more devious to not only walk up to her house and knock on her door, but to have the audacity to ask her for sugar knowing what he intended to do. Far more violent to threaten someone's life with a blade while you violate them.

Of course, as his daughter, he was never going to tell me this version of the story.

But learning what had really happened caused me to reevaluate every interaction and conversation I'd had with him with new eyes.

The most beneficial aspect of learning the truth was that I no longer trusted his assessment of me. It was harder to trust the judgment and proclamations of a person who would do such a thing.

It seemed nonsensical to let a person like that decide my worth and value.

Sometimes life will gift you with a beautiful, nicely wrapped revelation like the ones I've had of my parents. These flashes of insight allow us to see people and situations more clearly. These insights can also then become the catalyst for personal transformation that allows us to put a false narrative to rest.

But often the seeds of transformation are not so nicely gift-wrapped.

Usually it falls to us to figure out what's really going on. We have to sort the truth from illusion without much concrete evidence. Despite the lack of evidence, it can be done if we are willing to treat narratives as rumors and rely on our curiosity to open us up to the process of getting to know the truth.

A good example of a time when I had to decide for myself, without evidence, whether something was true about me or not is in my writing journey.

I knew I wanted to be a writer after I took my first creative writing class in college. Yet being the perfectionist I am, I set out to do everything *right*.

I was convinced that if I could just do everything right, then surely I would succeed.

The first right thing to do was get a degree in writing and literature. I got three, culminating in my MFA, which is something only *serious* writers do, or so I'd been told.

The second right thing to do was to publish. So I sent in my poems to literary journals and secured placements in respectable publications.

The third right thing to do was to write a novel and get an agent for it, because editors and publishing houses don't speak to lowly, no-name writers without one.

I finally finished a decent novel—after three failed attempts—and started sending out the manuscript to New York agents—the only *right* place to get an agent—and officially signed a contract with a reputable agent at a reputable agency.

The fact that I'd successfully jumped through so many hoops was supposed to be proof of my imminent overnight success.

I dove immediately into writing my next book while she, the agent, started trying to sell the first one to editors. I wanted to have my second book written and ready because I was convinced that it was only a matter of time before I saw my grand success play out on the stage.

Except that the agent wasn't able to sell the book. Or the second. Or the third.

I'd taken her advice, *just keep writing*, to heart as it was the *right* thing to do. But after three books which had not sold, I had to ask what was going on.

"Am I a bad writer? Do you just not want to tell me?" I asked.

I didn't think she would have agreed to be my agent if that's what she believed. Especially since agents don't get paid unless they sell your book. At this point, she'd been working for free as my agent for *four* years.

She assured me that it wasn't that I was a bad writer. The problem was that editors buy books they know how to sell. That's their job.

So if they don't know how to position a work in the market, they don't buy it.

Two of the most popular ways to position a debut writer (a writer who has never published before, as was the case for me here) is by genre or by voice.

If you walk into any bookstore and find the mystery section, you could pull any book off the shelf and know what you're getting. You may not know anything about the author or the story, but you will know plenty. That there's a crime. That someone will solve it. There is a certain recipe to the story. There are reader expectations that must be met. The same is true for romance. And for horror. We call this formula *genre*.

The second way to position an unknown writer is through voice or style. "If you love *<insert famous author name here>*, you'll love Kory M. Shrum."

You can also compare popular books rather than popular authors, such as, "If you loved Neil Gaiman's *Stardust* and V. E. Schwab's *Shades of Magic*, you'll love Kory M. Shrum's *Jack & the Fire Eater*."

Through comparison, fans of the more famous author or book will understand that they are likely to enjoy this book or author as well and give the unknown newbie a chance.

The only problem is that my fiction isn't formulaic. I write across genres and styles. I did back then, and I still do today. And my voice and style are unique too. Direct comparisons aren't easy to find.

So I asked my agent what we should do.

Because this was my dream, my *one* big dream—to be a published author. I was willing to do whatever it took to make that dream come true.

She suggested that I self-publish my book through Argo Navis, a self-publishing platform her agency was using at the time, and hope it did well enough that a larger publisher would pick it up.

Or I could write another book, but this time with a more formulaic story and more familiar voice and style.

I didn't like either of those options.

I loved that my stories were different. I didn't want to make them more like everyone else's. And I certainly didn't want to change my voice. It's *my* voice. It felt wrong to pretend to be like someone else.

But above all, I hated the idea of self-publishing. I'd already invested years in doing everything *right* so that I could prove my worth and legitimacy as an author.

I held the false narrative that self-published authors were losers who couldn't get traditional publishing deals.

And here I was, proving to be a loser who couldn't get a traditional publishing deal!

(It never occurred to me that quite a few famous authors had in fact self-published some or all of their work.)

In this moment, I was surrounded by unpleasant decisions on all sides. And in this discomfort, I was reminded of a shattering moment when I was twelve years old.

My father had picked me up from school and brought me home. I don't remember exactly what we'd been talking about, but let's pretend it was my grades. That will make it easier to share the accurate experience of what happened next.

As he parked in the driveaway, I dutifully handed over my report card.

He opened it up.

He looked at it.

He closed it and handed it back to me.

Then he said, "Kory, I think no matter what you do, no matter how hard you work, or how much you achieve academically, you're never going to be any better than your mother."

The report card may or may not have happened, but those were certainly his exact words.

And they devastated me.

Here I was, twelve years old, and so desperate for my father's love and approval, and it was the one thing he continually denied me.

But the real tragedy of his words was that it planted in me a seed, a false narrative, that no matter what I did, no matter how hard I worked, there was a limit to what I could do, what I could achieve.

And now, as I watched my dream of being a published author swim away from me, it felt like he was right about me.

Because I'd done everything right. I'd taken every step that I'd needed to take, I'd made all the right choices, I'd made all the right sacrifices, but here I was being told, *again*, that I wasn't good *enough*.

Here, several false narratives needed to perish in order for me to move past this moment. My prejudice around self-publishing was only one of them.

Another was that if I did everything right, if I was perfect, I would be chosen. That if I excelled at competing by the rules of someone else's game—whether it be my father's game, a publisher's, anybody's— I would be deemed *enough*.

A third false narrative that his words had planted was that there would always be a limit to what I could achieve. That, as he had put it, no matter what I did or how hard I worked, there was an upper limit to what I could do.

That's a rumor he started about me. And one that I believed with my whole twelve-year-old heart for decades to come.

Now there's *some* truth in it, if we consider outlandish ideas like lifting a two-ton truck. I will never be able to do *that*.

But when it comes to my dreams, when it comes to the things I want for myself, when it comes to how happy, how peaceful, how strong, how loving, how capable, how adaptable, how resilient, how kind, how brave, how loved, how flexible, how *free* I can be—there is no limit.

If I had believed my father's assigned narrative, I would have given up on my publishing dream then and there with a third unpublished book dead in the water. If I had accepted that the only *real* writers are traditionally published, I would have stopped writing.

Let me tell you what would *not* have happened if I had kept believing the rumors my father had created about me.

I would not have gone on to write over thirty books. I would have quit after those early failed attempts.

I would not have hit the *USA TODAY* bestseller list.

And I would not have sold over seven hundred thousand copies of my books.

I would have never come to believe that it's okay to do what you love for the simple fact that you love it.

I don't share these milestones to impress you. I just want to be clear how false narratives hold us back from finding the success and happiness we desire.

False narratives will hold us back and keep us small if we let them.

I played by my father's rules for so long because whenever I stood out, whenever I shone, I was punished for it. His love was withheld. And when I was young, to have his love and approval meant more to me then than being happy and whole.

If you are currently feeling stuck in any area of your life, there is a high probability that there is a false narrative that's got you hung up.

When it came to moving my publishing goals forward, I had to let go of the false narratives I was holding on to.

I also had to let go of my preconceptions around self-publishing, and what it would say about me if I chose that path.

I had to get curious about what I could achieve if I stopped letting everyone else write the story.

Let it be the same for you.

Let the false narrative, the rumor, be what dies. Let these burdensome ideas that hold you back disintegrate from your life. You don't need them anyway. They're keeping you chained to your fears.

The triumph you're looking for is on the other side of your fear.

If there's a story or a rumor that you believe about yourself, let it go.

Let that story go and write a new one.

That's your right, your power, and your privilege.

You say where your story ends. No one else.

Key Chapter Takeaways

- False narratives, whether self-imposed or imposed by others, can deeply affect our relationship with ourselves and our lives.
- If you're currently feeling stuck in an area of your life, there's likely a false narrative that's to blame. Identify it and work to unravel it as soon as possible.
- Awareness and curiosity are key to challenging and dissolving false narratives. Questioning the truth of these stories empowers us.
- Discovering the truth about yourself and past experiences is crucial for personal growth and building self-trust.

MANAGING FEAR

The degree to which you manage your fear will be the degree to which you experience success. Before you ask, no, there is no avoiding fear altogether.

Fear is part of the healing process. As unpleasant as pain, heartbreak, and loss can be, many of us are more comfortable with these emotions than the less familiar feelings of freedom, joy, and happiness. That's why it's important to know how to manage fear during the healing process. Any of these feelings, both positive and negative, can trigger fearful responses in us.

It's true that trauma creates and amplifies fear. If you've survived any sort of difficult situation, the rest of your life will become a lesson in learning how to relax in the presence of your fears—fear that it might happen again, fear that something worse will happen, fear that catastrophe might strike at any time.

It's a challenge, learning to relax in the presence of fear, but it can be done.

Fear is an emotion that even the bravest people experience.

If you are a brave person, I wager you've encountered a great deal of fear. You can't develop bravery in the absence of fear because one teaches us the other.

If, like me, you admire brave people, then you admire people who have learned how to manage their fear. What they have *not* done is get rid of it.

I've often been called brave by friends, but also by people who have never met me, which is often surprising to me considering that I feel like I'm the biggest coward I know.

For the longest time I thought, *Oh, people are just saying that because I've tricked them. I put up a strong front and it has created the illusion that nothing rattles me.*

But when I'm stoic (I'm not always, by the way), it's because of my trauma conditioning.

When I was a little girl and something awful happened like my mother having a breakdown, or I was left alone in a dangerous situation with unpredictable and inebriated people, or if my father threatened me with "I'll give you something to cry about," hundreds of experiences like this taught me that showing my fear was a liability. Showing fear usually made the situation worse.

Many abusers feel stronger when you act afraid. It emboldens them. It provokes them to hurt you more. My uncle was certainly one who liked to try to make people in the room cower away from him. He used his large frame to threaten and intimidate others.

Because this was the language of my family, I learned to project a cool facade when the situation got scary. The more dangerous the situation, the calmer my exterior.

By the time I was an adult, that stoicism presented itself in other dangerous situations. When my car hydroplaned before rolling three times in a ditch on a rainy afternoon, when a spider went *into* my mouth. At moments like that, people have said, "Wow, you're super calm. I'd be freaking out right now."

Oh, I *was* freaking out. I was just freaking out *inside*.

While my repeated exposure to upheaval and chaos and violence might have taught me how to project calm in difficult situations because everyone else was losing their mind around me, it didn't erase the fear.

Because fear is natural. There is no way to train the fear away.

We can only master it through management.

To have strong fear management means that that fear doesn't control your behavior.

It doesn't stop you from doing what you want to do.

It doesn't keep you doing things you know you should stop.

That's it. That's fear*less*ness.

How we become brave and fearless is a matter of skill. Anyone can get good at managing their fear. You can be shaking in your boots, ready to poop yourself, stress sweating, and still show up and do *the thing*—whatever *the thing* is.

Before I get too far ahead of myself here, and before I make it sound like I'm advocating stressing yourself out or even retraumatizing yourself for the sake of being fearless, let me talk about why there is no shame when you aren't ready to do something.

Overcoming fear is not about being hard on yourself. Please don't forget everything I've said about self-care as self-punishment.

Learning to manage your fear should not be self-punishment.

When I was eight years old my father picked me up and threw me in the deep end of a swimming pool. He did this so I would stop being afraid of the water.

I almost drowned and had to be rescued.

I became even more terrified of the water.

Don't throw yourself in the deep end when working with fear. There is no need to traumatize or retraumatize yourself. You don't have anything to prove to anybody here.

Forcing myself to do something even when it scares me should not feel like a punishment for some perceived weakness. Instead, I only confront fear when it is standing between me and something I care about, or a positive result that I want. Even then, I am very patient with myself.

When we aren't patient with ourselves, when we push for progress too hard and too quickly, it can backfire and create more fear like when my father threw me in the pool. This is the opposite of what we want.

In the case of fear, going slowly will actually help us progress more quickly.

When I was fifteen and learning how to drive, a common rite of passage, something awful happened. I was spending the day with my dad and one of his employees, riding around and completing his work errands.

Between stops, he turned to me and asked if I wanted to practice driving. Of course I said yes, and was really excited about it. What fifteen-year-old doesn't want to practice driving?

At the time, my dad drove a huge truck. I don't know if you know what a two-ton dually is, but it is a very large pickup truck. They're so big that they have extra tires in the back, four rear tires instead of two. Mind you, I am *maybe* five foot tall and not even a hundred pounds when this happens. I can't even really see over the steering wheel.

My father tried to adjust the wheel for me and gave me a phone book to sit on. When everything was ready, I hopped behind the steering wheel. I was pumped. I was *ready*.

"Okay. Back up," he said.

I looked at the steering wheel. I looked at the controls. They meant nothing to me.

I had never driven a car before, let alone a huge truck.

He said it again. "Come on, put it in reverse. Back it up."

"I don't know how," I said.

That's it.

That's all I said.

"I don't know how."

Apparently, this was the wrong thing to say. Because he started screaming at me, telling me I'm stupid, that I'm an idiot, that I don't know how to do anything. He cut me down as he had hundreds of times before until I began crying. I was crying not because of his callous words, which at that point I was growing somewhat used to. I was crying because I was embarrassed to be yelled at in front of someone else. For someone else to hear just how little he thought of me.

From this one experience, I have since carried with me a fear of learning anything new.

I don't like not knowing how to do something perfectly and immediately without effort. Many people feel this way. It is hardly unique to me.

It's normal to be nervous when trying something new.

But I don't get nervous. I get *terrified*. A sick to my stomach, I want to die kind of scared.

My heart will pound. My throat goes tight. My thoughts blurred. My arms heavy. I'll start stress sweating.

Sometimes I'll even get bitchy or angry and say something like, "I don't want to do this. It's dumb," which is only an attempt to hide the fact of how scared I am.

My physiological response and the anxiety that arises whenever I must be a beginner are outsized.

This is problematic because life is full of beginner moments.

Absolutely brimming with them.

This is the kind of fear I'm willing to confront and manage because this is the kind of fear that will keep me from really living.

I *can't* be scared of trying new things if I want to live my life.

This kind of fear will keep me from knowing who I really am and what I'm really capable of.

That's why I call this kind of fear problematic. And when something is problematic, address it.

For the longest time I thought I hated learning because of this fear response. Slowly I began to realize I actually love learning things.

I'm a curious person. I like accumulating skills and knowledge. I like novelty and surprise. This is the real me. The negative experience I had around being a beginner splintered me from my true self.

We can't have that.

It was through shadow work around fear that I was able to start to understand why I was so afraid of not knowing how to do something immediately and perfectly. Shadow work showed me why I was so uncomfortable asking for help or letting others teach me, guide me.

As mentioned in the shadow work section, the reason why we explore our shadows is because it isn't only bad stuff locked up in there. It's good stuff too.

When I started to *gently* explore my fear around being a beginner, I was able to see the gifts locked away from me as a result of that unhealed shadow.

I discovered that in truth, who I really was was not some anxious mess when it came to new things. The real me loved to learn when she felt safe to do so.

I like learning languages and art. How to draw and paint. I like learning how to fix things around the house. I replaced an entire toilet all by myself and built a six-foot high, seventy-foot-long privacy fence. I don't recommend that last one though. It hurt my back. Digging is a skill I could have passed on.

Two out of ten. Do not recommend.

(Two points for the coolness of being handy.)

All the same, my life would be immensely empty if I'd spent it avoiding being a beginner.

Be open to the idea that your fear hides who you really are from yourself, and that it hides what you're capable of.

It's true that fear is important. Fear is meant to keep us safe, and that's why we experience it. It's good to be afraid of the giant jaguar that might jump on your back, crack open your skull with one crunch of its jaw—fear is useful when it comes to waking us up and keeping us alert.

But fear can get confused sometimes.

It can tell you something is unsafe just because your heart was broken the last time you tried it, or because you were humiliated in front of others, or because someone who you loved abandoned you.

We have to keep reminding our mind that a jaguar is not the same threat level as a thirty-minute Spanish lesson, or a visit to the doctor.

Something might be hard or embarrassing, but I won't *actually* perish, even if I make a fool of myself.

By getting out of our comfort zone and experiencing "safe" fear through high-gain, low-risk activities, fear is one way to help us build confidence in ourselves and our abilities.

We can also explore our fears through honesty, trust, respect, and open communication. Yes, the same components that make up our relationship with ourselves. Because managing fear is part of the relationship.

To be honest with yourself when exploring fear means admitting to yourself that you're afraid. Why not? No one else is listening, and if you can't be honest with yourself about being scared shitless, who can you be honest with?

Admitting that something scares you, and admitting that the fear you're feeling might be pushing you away from something you want, will weaken fear's power over you.

This interruption will lessen habits like procrastination out of fear, because you will be able to see more clearly what you're doing because you're afraid.

After accepting that you are afraid, you will have an opportunity to practice trusting yourself in the face of your fear.

This may sound like "I trust that there is a reason this scares me. But I also don't believe that this fear is bigger or more powerful than I am. I trust myself to deal with this. I trust myself to hold the reins on my behavior until this fear passes."

The reason why I say "I trust there is a reason" is because not everyone can remember what happened to them that created the root of a fear. I am sure there are awful things that have happened to me that I don't remember. On one hand I'm grateful for that. On the other hand, it's upsetting because I can't imagine how much worse something must have been in order to be forgotten when I already remember so much terribleness.

If you have a fear but you have no specific memory attached to it and can't remember anything like it happening before, that is not an excuse to be mean to yourself about it. Remember how important it is to speak to yourself kindly. Telling yourself that you're silly or stupid to be afraid of something is not kind.

And yet we treat ourselves like this all the time.

We tell ourselves what we are and aren't allowed to be afraid of.

Whatever scares you, that's your fear.

Don't add that extra layer of self-punishment or self-rejection to it. Trust your instincts even when you don't understand them.

Affirm yourself. And believe that you have the power to move past fear and toward the thing you really want anyway.

Respect, the third crucial relationship component in the context of fear, means having a healthy respect for your fear, but also a boundary.

Respect what your fear is trying to tell you, about yourself and about a situation. Fear can provide us a lot of juicy information about who we really are and where we need to do the work. Fear is usually our first clue that shadow work needs to be done.

But we can also respectfully decline to be led around on a leash by fear.

Open communication is about how you talk to yourself when you are afraid. This is perhaps the most crucial aspect of working with fear.

Fear has a loud, booming voice.

When we are afraid, we must be louder.

When I started speaking publicly, I was definitely out of my comfort zone. Many people share a fear of getting up on stage and having countless strangers staring back at you while the bright lights beam down from above.

But I also knew I was meant to do it. It was important to me to become the kind of person who spoke up for and helped others.

When I'm afraid, the most helpful thing I can do is speak to my fears the same way that I would speak to a scared child that I love.

Fear: "What if they don't like me? What if I'm bad at it? What if I mess up? What if everyone thinks I'm stupid? What if I ruin everything and they never let me try again?"

Me, speaking to fear: "What are you talking about! They're going to love you. You've worked really hard! You practiced so much! You're going to do a great job! And even if you make little mistakes, it's no big deal. It only matters that you have fun. Look how brave you are getting up there and telling stories. Not a lot of people could do that, but you are. I'm so proud of you."

It felt ridiculous the first few times I tried to be my own cheerleader. There was a small swell of grief that I didn't have someone like a parent to say these things to me instead, as my father was incapable and my mother was dead.

But once I moved past this self-pity, I recognized there were many people in my life who were happy to encourage me.

Most importantly, that it was my job to encourage myself and there was no shame in doing so.

The same will be true for you working through your fears.

Continue speaking to yourself as kindly and frequently as you need to in order to keep yourself moving through fear.

Don't give yourself a hard time for being afraid.

Often we think it's okay to be hard on ourselves just because we grew up. I heard a lot of "Toughen up, get over it, you're too old to act like this" growing up—and I was an *actual* child.

Don't give that kind of dismissive and demeaning radio play in your head. Set a boundary in place against it. Do not tolerate it or entertain it. And don't, for a second, believe it.

And if it still seems silly, speaking kindly to yourself, I will only add this:

Speaking to myself the same way my abusers and bullies spoke to me never did me any favors.

It didn't make me achieve more. It didn't make me more capable or efficient. It sure as hell didn't help me connect with my power or strength.

All it did was slow me down and hold me back.

To Be Friendly With Fear

Working with fear not only gives us a chance to improve on our relationship with ourselves—through honesty, trust, respect, and open communication—it also gives us an opportunity to build up tolerance to fear.

We won't make fear go away completely. That's a fool's errand.

But treating fear like an outspoken and somewhat overbearing friend will make us stronger. With practice, we will develop the muscles we need to handle fear with ease whenever it arrives because at the end of the day, fear management is just another skill.

Every time we confront and overcome a fear, we'll get braver. We'll gain courage and confidence. We'll also be weakening those destructive thought patterns and self-criticism by interrupting them with a louder voice of our own.

Many of the techniques explored earlier in this book such as breath work, meditation, mindfulness, mental de-escalation, curiosity, awareness, and dispelling false narratives are all techniques you can use against fear.

Like any strong emotion, you will disempower your fear once you stop feeding it.

Better still, when you manage your fear, you're practicing self-love, self-confidence, and self-trust. You're getting better and better at mental de-escalation. You're also honing your intuition.

Is It Intuition or Fear?

Intuition is an instinctive feeling we all experience. Depending on what kind of experiences you've had or trauma you've endured, your intuition may be more or less intact. For me, because I was raised by a narcissistic parent, my intuition took major damage. His repetitive undermining of my thoughts, beliefs, and worldview taught me to always second-guess myself.

The hypervigilance of navigating dangerous environments also taught me to always expect the worst.

This is an unhelpful combination for connecting with one's intuition.

However, trusting ourselves, trusting our intuition specifically, is a big part of having a great relationship with ourselves. But for some of us, we will have to relearn how to connect with and utilize our intuition. This will be especially true if you were taught to deny, mistrust, or devalue your intuition and instincts.

The distinction between intuition and fear is difficult to draw. It's certainly more of an art than a science. It also may not be immediately clear, the connection between intuition and wellness, so let me begin there.

When I say intuition, I'm referring to our ability to understand or know something without conscious reasoning or evidence. Sometimes this is described as a gut feeling or instinctive understanding of a situation.

Intuition can come into play in various areas of our lives, whenever we rely on decision-making, problem-solving, creativity, and navigating interpersonal relationships. Just from this short list, you can likely see the pillars of mind & emotions, spirit, and connection, but it's also present in the body pillar because in the body is where we register intuitive feelings.

There is some debate about what intuition actually is. Some people believe that intuition is a form of unconscious processing of information based on past experiences. Others see it as a more mystical or spiritual phenomenon.

In the context of managing fear, recognizing your intuition *as* intuition is important.

Distinguishing between intuition and anxiety can be challenging because they can sometimes feel similar, especially in situations where there is uncertainty and high emotional tension. Also, it often feels like intuition and fear are reading from the same cue cards.

When your inner voice cries, *Don't do it!*, who said that? Intuition or fear?

But there are ways to figure out if the voice in your head is truly your instinctual feelings or if it's only fear talking.

First of all, the physical experience of each is different.

When I'm connected to intuition, something feels right. I feel calm and certain rather than the electric, jittery feelings of fear and anxiety. They are also registered in different parts of the body. I always know I'm anxious, for example, because my arms, especially my biceps, will begin to feel as heavy as wet bags of sand. My intuition never gives me wet-sand arms.

When I *know* something intuitively, there is a clear confidence in that knowing. Because of this clear knowing, I don't tend to escalate the strong emotions. If I am catastrophizing in my head, imagining the situation getting worse and worse and *worse*, that's usually a sign that it's fear talking, not intuition.

Overthinking, second-guessing, confusion, those are all signs that it's fear whispering to you, not your true inner compass.

If I'm obsessed about time, that is also usually fear. Fear often increases the sense of urgency by running a countdown clock while it's harassing me.

Intuition, on the other hand, seems to have an immortal's sensibility. There is no rush, no urgency with intuition. It has been my experience that intuition is more focused on my long-term goals. It's more oriented toward my life's purpose and direction, not on the immediate concerns.

Intuition seems to be of the mind that it doesn't matter how long it takes us to get somewhere or do something. What must get done will get done.

As I said, knowing the difference between intuition and fear is more of an art than a science, and will get better with practice. And it's okay if you get it wrong sometimes. I still do myself. But you can develop the ability to distinguish between intuition and fear until their voices are clearly distinct more often than not.

Finding ourselves steeped in fear is always an opportunity to practice honing the ability to know the difference. It's our chance to learn how to listen to ourselves even in difficult moments—which is a powerful skill.

When we start listening, we might hear things like "I'll never be okay. They're right about me. I'm worthless. I'm weak. I can't do this."

Your intuition would never say such things to you. That's fear talking.

Over time this internal voice can be trained to speak louder than the critical voice. How?

If we believe the supportive voice, if we give it our attention, it will get stronger and more powerful than the fearful one. For most of us, the fearful one is louder because that is the one we've been believing in and investing in for a long time. We will have to consciously change that if we want to shift the balance of power within us.

It can be especially challenging because sometimes positive, loving thoughts feel just as scary—sometimes even more scary than the negative ones. But if we remain committed to the habit of speaking kindly to ourselves, our true inner compass will get stronger.

Rarely do we receive our desires on the first try. And the harder we try and the more we fail, the more we get discouraged. With enough discouragement in our hearts, hope can feel like a liability. To get our hopes up feels like setting ourselves up for more heartbreak.

However, just because we don't succeed at something the first time doesn't mean our intuition was wrong, or that we aren't meant to have something.

I've discovered that my own intuition will always lead me down the path that's right for me—but it doesn't mean that path will be free of failure. Our intuition isn't afraid of failure the way we are. So if you encounter failure, it doesn't mean your inner voice led you astray.

Failure is a refinement process. Each failed attempt improves our approach and clarifies our vision. Treat failure simply as feedback and not as an excuse to doubt yourself.

By continuing to confront our fears in spite of setbacks, we have the opportunity to strengthen that self-trust.

Is Your Fear Useful?

One of the problems with unmanaged fear is that it can stop me from doing what is good for me. For example, there's a book—a series of books, actually—that I really, *really* want to write but I haven't started. I haven't even sketched down my ideas about it because I'm so nervous. Fear says, *If you write the book now, you're going to ruin the great story in your head. You're just not skilled enough to tell a story like that.*

Listening to this fear has me putting off beginning the project in favor of less intimidating projects.

In this example, fear is a hindrance, not a help. This kind of fear is standing between me and something I want, something that would lead me toward the creative freedom and growth that I desire for myself.

Good fear hones our focus. It makes us sit up and pay attention. It makes us double down and invest harder in the success of something.

It's a subtle distinction between *good* fear and *bad* fear, but this understanding makes a world of difference in how we work with our fear.

How do we distinguish between useful fear and unhelpful fear?

Here is a clarifying question I ask myself:

How do I feel after I do the thing that scares me?

How I feel afterward is a good indicator of whether it's useful fear or unhelpful fear.

For example, when I was training for my black belt, I never actually wanted to go to the dojo. I had immense anxiety about it even though I studied Uechi-Ryu for many years.

It didn't matter how many times a week I went, I always showed up with knots in my stomach and sweaty palms. But after every class I would feel amazing. I'd always be glad I'd gone.

Working with that fear made me stronger. It made me focused. That is a useful kind of fear.

The fears keeping me from tackling an ambitious creative project —not so useful. When I have the opportunity to begin the project but I pass on it yet again, I don't feel good about that. That's one of my clues that I'm holding myself back from something I want and would love to experience.

It's how you feel afterward that matters, rather than before.

The next time you find yourself in this fearful space, ask yourself how you feel after you made your decision or did the scary thing. If you felt good afterward, if the experience perked you up and dialed in your focus, excellent. Keep doing the scary thing and let the useful fear it produces build your self-confidence. If you felt bad after you did it, maybe the choice wasn't right for you. Maybe you're not ready or that's not what you genuinely want.

If you want to be a well cared for human, keep working with your fears. Keep trying to understand them through de-escalation, meditation, mindfulness, and introspection. The more you practice turning toward your fear, the more it will teach you about who you are, what you want, and how to refine your efforts.

Key Chapter Takeaways

- Fear is natural and unavoidable. It is an emotion that even the bravest people must face.
- Bravery is developed through experiencing and managing fear, not through the absence of it. Brave people have learned to manage fear, not eliminate it.

- Effective fear management means that fear doesn't control your behavior or stop you from pursuing your dreams.
- Respecting fear means understanding its purpose and the insight it provides, while also setting boundaries to not let it control your life.
- Exploring your fears through shadow work can help reveal your hidden strengths.
- You must strengthen your own positive self-talk until its voice is louder than your fear's.
- Mental self-care techniques like de-escalation, mindfulness, breathwork, introspection, and dispelling false narratives are all options for you to use when working with fear.

DEVOTION, NOT DISCIPLINE

As a rule, I don't like the word *discipline*. It makes me think of hard, unforgiving people. Rigid people. And I'm pretty sure this connection comes from the fact that my father often hid his abuse behind the word *discipline*. "Oh, I'm just trying to make you more disciplined. I'm doing this to you because you need to be more disciplined." Yet whatever action he was pairing with these words was abusive.

My negative view of what it meant to be disciplined was reinforced by media—movies, TV, books, stories of all kinds—in which disciplined people must endure blood, sweat, tears, and general misery in order to succeed.

I had enough blood, sweat, and tears going on, thanks.

I'm not saying that blood, sweat, and tears aren't often part of success, but these depictions made discipline so unattractive. There was not a single part of me that wanted to be bloody, sweaty, or tearful anymore.

This is likely why it took me so long to realize that there is a better way to develop discipline. And that this more loving, kinder form of discipline was no less effective. In fact, I've found it to be more effective than being hard on myself.

Discipline is an act of self-care. An act of self-love.

Discipline can be framed as devotion to yourself, rather than a way to whip yourself into shape.

Just as we should avoid using self-care as self-punishment, we can also avoid using discipline as self-punishment.

Devotion can be used to motivate you and help you stay committed to the big changes you envision for your life. Devotion is a commitment to the promises you make to yourself. Devotion is also a commitment to the dream you have for yourself.

Self-discipline is our ability to control our impulses and behaviors in order to achieve our goals. Our ability to remain patient and committed to a vision and the willingness to endure temporary discomfort for the sake of that grander vision is self-discipline. When we talk about getting focused, when we talk about time management, or resisting distraction or temptation, that's self-discipline.

When we have a certain set of unspoken rules, there are things we will or won't do for our own good. Our non-negotiables. Whether or not we adhere to these rules reflects how disciplined we are. Perhaps you declare, "I'm not going to smoke because it's bad for me. I'm not going to drink because it makes me depressed. I'm not going to get into screaming matches with my mother because…" Your ability to keep these promises to yourself and control your behavior accordingly reflects how disciplined you are.

In media, movies, and TV, when someone is demonstrating these tremendous feats of mental or physical training, such as martial artists, boxers, athletes, or dream chasers of any kind, including artists, writers, entrepreneurs, and musicians—we see their devotion to an outcome or dream through the actions they take.

It is hard to remain devoted to yourself in a way that accepts and loves yourself as you are today and also wishes for growth and self-improvement.

You are enough and there is room for improvement. Both of these statements can be true at the same time. And these entwined ideas lie at the center of what it means to practice self-discipline as devotion.

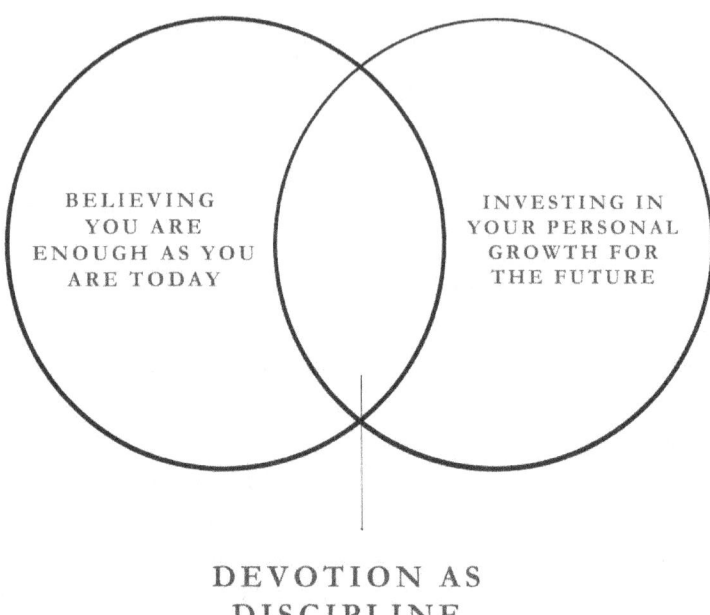

How can we approach discipline as a form of self-devotion that doesn't rely on the brutal, heavy-handed methods we often associate with the word *discipline*? How can we make sure we don't slip into self-punishment?

As with most things, it may first require a mindset shift. Do you have negative associations with the word like I did? Anything that may stop you from approaching the idea of discipline with positivity?

For a long time I resisted the idea of being a disciplined person because I thought of it as too controlling. Looking at all the ways I wasn't measuring up or behaving well enough had me feeling bad about who I was and what I was capable of.

But this was really to my detriment because discipline teaches us so many valuable skills, especially when it is a balanced, patient approach to our self-care.

Self-discipline teaches us:

- Self-control
- Focus and concentration
- Time management
- Consistency
- Resilience
- Responsibility
- How to finish things
- Habit formation
- Confidence and empowerment

For me, the first step was overcoming my negative perception of discipline. Realizing, ah, maybe what my abusive father did wasn't discipline. I had to warm up to the idea that my rejection of all forms of structure was due to my chronic exposure to someone controlling, and that aversion might not be so useful to me.

Once I realized that actually I can benefit from discipline, especially if I view it as devotion to my own evolution, I made progress.

There are many reasons why you might resist the idea of discipline. It could be a difficult background like mine with a highly disciplinary parent or caregiver. Or perhaps you had other negative past experiences, with someone criticizing you, telling you how you're not good enough and how you need to shape up.

You may have encountered failure once or a hundred times and it created a narrative that it doesn't matter how disciplined you are, it won't work out for you anyway. Failure and setbacks can be demotivating, and it's hard to be disciplined without motivation.

If we aren't clear on our *why*, on our reason for investing in ourselves and being disciplined, it will be challenging to continue to persevere. We could also be overwhelmed by the amount of change we seek and not know where to start.

We may also be addicted to instant gratification. I've yet to meet anyone who *loves* being patient, but discipline asks us to be.

Whatever the reason, if you can recognize that you have an aversion to the idea of discipline or even the word *discipline*, I'd start there. Look at that more closely and figure out what's going on that might be stopping you from getting started before you even begin.

Once you explore these ideas in your journal or simply have a good think about them (I call this contemplation or self-analysis), let's take that self-reflection and awareness a bit further.

Take time to reflect on your current level of discipline. Identify areas where you struggle with consistency, focus, or motivation.

Understand your strengths, weaknesses, habits, and triggers that influence your ability to stay disciplined. These are all aspects of discipline that you can explore to clarify your relationship with and view of discipline. Just be sure that you are doing it in a way that is not self-punishing or self-critical, which comes down to how you speak about yourself and what your intentions behind the action are.

At the end of the day, self-discipline is an act of self-love. You make a promise to your future self. That you are going to heal. That you are going to get stronger, happier, and healthier.

Self-discipline is keeping the promises you make to *you*.

That's a big deal. You can hold that vision, that dream that you have for yourself. You can keep moving toward it. And you can do it lovingly by speaking to yourself positively, by cheering yourself on, by focusing on the wins and not the losses. By being your own biggest fan.

And just know that discipline is a muscle. The more you use it, the easier it will be to be disciplined. Just keep at it. Keep showing up for yourself.

Every time you do, you're communicating to yourself that you're someone who deserves commitment. You are someone who deserves to have promises kept and needs honored. Treating yourself this well will make it difficult to accept bad, disrespectful behavior from others.

Never forget that you deserve nothing less.

. . .

Key Chapter Takeaways

- Discipline is an act of self-care and self-love.
- Self-discipline as devotion says that you are enough as you are and there is room for improvement.
- Self-devotion is more effective than discipline as self-punishment. Self-punishment only undermines our sense of self-worth and demotivates us.
- Self-discipline teaches us to trust ourselves and depend on ourselves as well as many useful skills such as self-control, focus, concentration, and patience.
- Self-discipline is a promise you make to your future self. Keeping that promise will not only transform your life, but it will build self-trust and self-respect.

ONE FOR THE HELPERS

I recently completed a speaking engagement, and after the event, a young woman came up to me and thanked me for speaking. She said a few kind words about the presentation and what she liked and so on, which I appreciated. Then she asked me this: "But how do I bring up the subject of wellness with others?"

For a bit of context, it might help to know that she was in the health care industry, and that she was seeing the signs of burnout and stress in her clinic and was wondering how to initiate that conversation with her coworkers. She wanted to share what she'd learned with me that day with them.

First of all, I love that. I love that for some of us, our instinct is to take what we learn and use it to help other people. The world would be a better place if this was everyone's first instinct.

Secondly, I didn't want to, but I knew I had to answer her question honestly.

My policy of honesty, trust, respect, and open communication isn't just for myself. I try, when at all possible, to have the same standards for my relationships with all others—be they strangers or my dearest friends.

Sometimes being honest is hard. But I will still tell you the truth now.

You can't make other people take care of themselves.

I learned this the hard way with all my years as my mother's daughter. All the ways I had tried and failed to take care of her, to protect her, or even marginally improve the quality of her life.

Sometimes it's a matter of not having enough resources. Sometimes it's a matter of not having the right system in place that makes the healing possible. Both were certainly true for my mother.

When I left her at the end of the driveway, even though I knew I was choosing to save the only life I could at that time—my own—I was still secretly wishing things could be different.

Some people are not ready to heal.

Sometimes this is because of where they are mentally or emotionally. Sometimes this is because they need larger, systemic help—like from a functioning mental health care system—which we don't currently have in place.

Does this mean we should give up on people?

No.

Should we stop loving people or caring about people?

Absolutely not.

But we will have to accept our limitations in any given situation.

It's very normal when we start doing self-work, and start feeling better as a result of our efforts, to want to evangelize to others about how amazing our new program, plan, regime, etc., is.

I mean, I wrote this entire book for similar reasons. I'm no better.

But we will never be able to *make* someone better by our will and enthusiasm alone.

We can fight for change, for a world that makes healing easier—as easy as it can be—but we must also accept that transformation is always in the hands of the individual.

They must want to change.

And many people don't want to, because they are afraid, because of false narratives and limiting beliefs—for a million personal reasons.

Of course my secret wish is that by this point in the book I have made healing as exciting and enticing an opportunity as I possibly can —but I still must accept the possibility that once you have read this, you will close the book, put it down, and then do absolutely nothing at all.

I must make my peace with that, knowing full well that many times in my life, I have received *very* good, *very* helpful advice from loving, wise souls—and then immediately did nothing at all. Or worse, I did the opposite.

People must be ready to heal. *And* they must have the resources to do so. Both conditions must be met and at the same time. I don't think I need to tell you that often they are not.

That doesn't mean you can't try to help, though.

Plenty of people tried to help me when I wasn't ready, and I still believe I benefited from their efforts if only because they introduced me to new ideas and possibilities I'd never considered.

They planted seeds that would sprout weeks, months, or years later.

So if you have someone in mind—a loved one, a friend, a coworker, anyone—then yes. Try to have that conversation with them. Maybe your concern will push them a little closer to being ready, if nothing else.

But as you try to help others, please keep the following in mind:

It's beautiful to be a helper, but never help at the expense of your own well-being.

Losing my mother the way I did, and telling my story afterward, has sown in me a strong desire to improve the lives of others. I may not always feel this way, but certainly at the time of writing this book, it feels like a lifelong mission, to put as much healing and love into the world as I can.

Yet I make this aspiration for the world at the same time that I make a promise to myself—I will help however and whenever I can, but never at the expense of my own well-being.

If I lose myself in the process, it will not be any different than when I lost myself in the struggle for my own mother's salvation all those years ago.

Codependency has many faces. Some personal, some larger in scale.

Make the same promise to yourself.

If help is needed and you can provide it, please do.

But if and when you can't, it's okay to put yourself first.

This doesn't mean you are a bad person.

It doesn't mean you're somehow failing or not measuring up.

It doesn't mean anything at all except that right now something else needs your time and attention more—and that something else is *you*.

You should always be your priority.

You will be of no use to anyone if you're not well yourself.

If you try to help someone and it doesn't work, don't sacrifice yourself in hopes of changing that outcome.

Retreat and live to fight another day.

Don't forget that there are two layers of healing and transformation.

There is preparation for healing and transformation. Then there is the healing and transformation itself. You will not necessarily know which stage a person is in when you offer to help them.

If you felt that you gave someone everything they needed to succeed and then they did not, do *not* take this to heart. It's very possible they are still preparing. If you've ever experienced healing or transformation yourself, certainly you must know that several internal shifts must occur before we're ready to do the work. And even when we're ready to do the work, maybe we are too under-resourced to do so —too tired, too overwhelmed, too burned out, or too paralyzed by fear.

How many times have you wanted to learn a new skill, or start a new exercise routine, or eat healthier, only to realize it was the fourth, fifth, or eighteenth try before you were able to make the change stick?

We must be willing to give others the same grace.

Healing is terrifying for many of us.

When I was a teenager, cliff jumping was all the rage.

There were limestone cliffs looking over a river, and you could leap off the edge into the water below.

It didn't matter how many times I saw my friends do this. It didn't matter how many times they leapt off, disappeared into the murky water, only to come up smiling and laughing.

It didn't matter how safe I knew I would be. It didn't matter how fun I knew it would be.

The idea of jumping off a cliff still scared the shit out of me.

I wanted to do it, but I also had to pump myself up to do it. Sometimes I had to false run toward the edge several times only to pull back at the last moment. Sometimes I had to jump off holding someone else's hand.

Healing is like this.

We love and fear the idea of healing in equal measure.

Pushing people off the cliff for their own good will never work. It can actually inhibit their progress by triggering more fear for them to work through.

It's best to let people find themselves at their own pace.

In the meantime, don't underestimate the power of your steady presence and consistent reassurances.

You may worry that this isn't enough.

I promise you that it is.

Don't be attached to outcomes.

There are many reasons why attachment to outcomes will only set us up for disappointment. Often because our ideas of what a person will look like healed may not in fact be the reality. Having expectations for a person and how they should live will only invite heartbreak. Leave room to be surprised.

Find the sweet spot between helpful and involved, but not overly invested.

Helpful and involved will be defined differently for each of us, depending on what we can give and where we are in our own healing process. For me, helpful and involved means providing as many resources as I can to others through stories, books, podcasts, speaking, and the like, as well as doing my best to mirror their innate goodness and my belief in their abilities back to them.

I also know that my best abilities lie in storytelling, teaching, communicating—and I use those skills to help others, and to protect things that I believe need protecting.

Know what you believe, and know what you can do.

Then give those parts of yourself freely and without reserve to the world because power is meant to be shared.

That will be your gift to the people around you.

But know also that success is not promised. Even progress isn't promised.

The most important thing is to give the gift.

Give, but know that the receiver is allowed to do what they please with it.

Don't take on responsibility that isn't yours.

For a long time I took on my mother's wellness as my own responsibility. Given the traditional structure of society, it's the mother who should be concerned with the child's well-being, but our roles were reversed. And as long as I held tight to and believed in that responsibility, I stayed unwell.

For the same reason, I caution you against assuming responsibility that isn't yours.

Your well-being is your responsibility. The well-being of others, unless you have a minor child, is not your responsibility.

It is your responsibility to put your gifts into the world, but it is not your responsibility to police how those gifts are used.

It is your responsibility to show up for yourself and in defense of justice, but you never need do so at the expense of your own wellness or life.

You can love and let go. It's hard, but it can be done.

It must be done.

Because as long as we remain entangled in each other's wounds, none of us will heal. The best thing we can do is untangle ourselves, one by one, and build ladders for others (better systems) as we go.

Five Ways to Help Others

Those five general principles I just outlined are good for any helpers who want to stay balanced and well while extending themselves to others. But if you're looking for tangible actions rather than general guiding principles, here are five strategies that you could use now:

Lead with yourself.

The woman who approached me after my keynote had great concern for her fellow health care workers. I recommended that she share her own concern *for herself* the next time there was an opportunity to do so.

In a staff meeting or over an email chain, she could say that she'd been reading about the high rate of burnout amongst their profession and admit to feeling the strain herself. This honesty and vulnerability might spark the conversation she was hoping for.

Or she could go to her superiors and ask if there were any wellness initiatives or resources for the workers of her clinic. From there she could make an effort to communicate what those resources were and how to access them to the rest of the team, making sure the others knew there was help if they needed it.

I recommend this you-first approach because no one wants to hear, "You look like you're struggling. Do you need my help?" Those of us who are truly struggling are also doing our best to hide it. To have it pointed out that not only are we unwell but we aren't even doing a good job of hiding it feels like adding insult to injury.

So lead with you. If you're willing to admit your own struggle, then that may open the conversation with others.

If they ask you what you've been doing, by all means share.

Letting their curiosity lead them to the information will have a higher rate of success than information you force upon them.

. . .

Set a good example.

This is a step away from leading with yourself. In the previous example, you're making a direct effort to initiate the wellness conversation, or to start others on a healing path. But it's possible they are not ready to have that conversation or do that work. Don't forget the two levels of transformational healing, after all.

If they are not yet ready, it might be more worth your time to simply demonstrate the power of transformation. Focus on your own healing and well-being and allow the people around you to witness your healing with their own eyes. That will be far more motivating than any pep talk or lecture you give someone.

Just be sure that you let your own results speak for themselves. Again, no one wants to be proselytized to.

Your intentions to help others should always come from a sincere place of wanting their lives to improve for their own sake. Any kind of self-righteous approach like "Oh, you poor thing, you're such a mess, let's get you sorted out" will almost certainly blow up in your face.

We are all equals here.

And not one of us is getting out of this alive, no matter how good we get at this game called life.

Share resources.

Speaking of providing resources, there are ways to do this more naturally. You could send an email or text with a link to an article or idea. *I just read this and it's fantastic.* Don't hound them to read it. Just send it their way and consider your work done.

Or perhaps when it's your turn to pick a book at the next book club, you choose one that focuses on wellness, as a more natural way to open the conversation.

Or if you hang out together with a friend in a coffee shop reading— as I sometimes do with my fellow introverted friends—you can read such a book in front of them. If they're curious, they will ask, and you can point them in the right direction or loan them the book.

If you talk about it, frame it carefully.

"Oh, I love this book because..." will be far more effective than "Oh, I definitely think *you* should read it. You need this advice *so* much."

What's important here is that you do not push, pressure, or preach. It's easy and tempting to do. But we can't tell people how to live their lives—says the person who wrote a self-help book about how to live a life.

All we can do is share what helped us most and hope that they will find it helpful too.

Invite them along.

Sometimes it really is easier to jump off a (hopefully metaphorical) cliff holding someone else's hand. Having an accountability buddy often leads to changes that stick. Usually.

Sometimes.

I had a lovely gym buddy in college, someone who is still dear to me to this day. And while we always showed up at the gym as agreed upon, we also sometimes left the gym to go eat ice cream instead of working out.

I'm not saying there is anything wrong with this. I'm only saying the results of this approach can be mixed.

That said, inviting the people you love to participate in self-care with you might be effective under the right circumstances.

You could say to your friend, "I'm struggling with my mental health these days. I want to start taking more walks for fresh air, exercise. Do you think you could join me? I could use the company."

Now they're doing you a favor and helping you out.

You've made it about you rather than making it about how you think they need to work on themselves, which would be a far less enticing offer. You're not telling them that they need to get out of the house more because you haven't seen them change out of those pajamas for five days straight.

This way you're making the work easier and more accessible. You're providing opportunities to practice self-care.

What you invite them to can be anything. Invite them to join a sports team with you. A club. A weekly yoga class. A cooking class. An art class. A book club. Anything that you think will benefit you both is on the table.

And healing is always more fun when we do it together.

Mirror their goodness.

One of the most important things we can do for others is to simply affirm their goodness and potential. So many of us are convinced that we aren't enough, and that nothing we do will ever be enough. That there is something fundamentally wrong with us that will never be fixed, no matter how hard we work at it.

Don't underestimate the power of being that one shining light for someone.

It took a great deal of kindness from others, affirmation and love from others, before I began to believe that it just might be true that I was a good person deserving of love and care.

My early life and experiences had not given me that belief.

But many loving and kind people who had passed through my life since did.

I was able to heal in large part because these souls mirrored the innate goodness in me, held that space patiently for me, until I began to see myself differently.

Plant those seeds in others whenever you can.

We plant these seeds through encouragement. Not toxic false positivity. We should never say, "Everything is totally great! You're fine!" when that is far from the truth.

We are still trying to be honest, after all.

But it hopefully isn't a lie to say, "I know you're struggling and not at your best right now, but I believe in you a thousand percent. I know you can do this. And I'll do whatever I can to help you."

Early in my therapy sessions, after a particularly disheartening session I admitted to my very kind therapist, Dr. A, that I felt like the most lost, confused, and messed-up person in the world.

"How long will it take?" I asked him. Truly I was begging, not asking. "How long will it take before I feel okay?"

That was my best hope—just okay. I couldn't even imagine the sort of life and freedom and love I've since received. I was in so much pain that I was desperate for *just okay*.

He considered me for a moment and then told me this story:

"When my son was little, he used to get very scared at night. We tried all sorts of things, night-lights, leaving the door open, you name it. But the only thing that helped him was if I sat on the end of his bed until he went to sleep. For weeks, he always asked me the same question: 'How long will you stay?' And I always gave him the same answer: 'For as long as it takes.' After a while he began to believe me. And that's when the fear went away."

What Dr. A was trying to help me see was that a large part of my struggle was the same as his son's. It was the fear that maybe things would never get better, that I would never get to *okay*, that was making my difficult situation even more difficult.

And the only way to assuage those fears was to sit with them for as long as it took.

This act of sitting with them rather than struggling with them is what helps the whole situation relax and dissolve for good.

We can do this for others.

We can be present and affirming, for as long as it takes. We can keep telling them how worthy they are. We can tell them who they really are until they start to believe it for themselves.

We can keep telling them how much they matter until they are finally able to relax enough for the healing to begin.

Key Chapter Takeaways

- It's important to help others, but never at the expense of ourselves. Without our own well-being in place, our efforts will be ineffective and counterproductive.
- We can't force people to take care of themselves or invest in their own relationship with themselves, no matter how important we believe the work to be.

- We must maintain a balance between giving and guiding, without being overbearing or condescending.
- It is important never to think we are further along or better than someone else just because they are struggling. Most people will sense this, and it will be counterproductive to their healing.
- One of the most loving and impactful ways to help someone heal is to simply mirror and affirm their innate worth.

ARE YOU READY?

I've given you a lot of information in the preceding chapters, but now I want to give you a blueprint for acting on that information. Otherwise, it may just live in your head and be useless to you. That's why this chapter is dedicated to clarifying how you can take the ideas I've introduced in this book and directly apply them to your life.

Let's break this blueprint down in steps:

The Three Steps to Establishing a Relationship With Yourself

Step one: Assess your relationship with yourself

The first step is to assess your relationship with yourself and the condition of your four pillars. We can't get to where we want to go if we don't know where we are. Right from the beginning, you will want to bring the four key ingredients into the mix. Start by being honest with yourself. Do you love yourself as you are today? Are you proud of who you are and your choices? What do you wish your life was like? Who do you wish you were?

Write these things down in your journal or type them up. You don't have to share them with anyone, so why not tell the truth? I hope I've made it clear that it's important not to lie to ourselves, especially when it comes to taking control of our lives, which is exactly what you're doing.

Respect whatever comes up for you in the assessment. The good, the bad, the beautiful, the ugly. All of your experiences and choices as still yours. Whatever you think you've done wrong or imperfectly, don't give yourself a hard time about it. That's in the past. If it's still happening now, that's okay too. You're already moving away from it even by doing this assessment.

Don't worry if you don't love what you find in this self-assessment. This is where I remind you that when I began, I was a highly depressed, addicted, anxious, self-loathing, confused, toxic little hot mess.

There's no tangle you can't get yourself out of. But we have to start by looking at those knots.

Step 2: Identify your pillar breakers
Don't forget the holy trinity of how you think about yourself, how you speak about yourself, and how you act toward yourself.

We want all of our hard work to amount to something. For that reason, it's important to know what we might be doing that destroys our own well-being. Which pillar breakers are undoing all of your hard work? Do you think mean thoughts about yourself? Do you say mean things about yourself? If so, prioritize breaking the habit of tearing yourself down.

Do you struggle with fear? Is your fear of certain situations or experiences controlling your behavior and cutting you off from your power and freedom? Are you entrapped by a sense of obligation? Do you have a toxic person in your life who *counts* on that sense of obligation in order to extract free emotional or physical labor out of you?

Do you have any shame that needs addressing?

Do you use self-care as self-punishment? As more proof that you're not good enough and you need to whip yourself into shape ASAP?

What stories do you tell yourself about yourself? Are they true? And even if they are, are they kind?

Which of these pillar breakers—negativity, FOG, shame, self-punishment, or false narratives—are interfering with your ability to build a strong relationship with yourself?

See that.

Write it down.

Again, all personal transformation begins with awareness. If we can't clearly see the ways in which we hurt ourselves, we can't put a stop to it.

So don't lie to yourself here either. None of that, "Well, yeah, I say mean things about myself but so does everyone. It's not really a problem, is it? Well, yeah, my narcissistic mother has me believing the story that I'm a selfish, self-serving asshole, but that story probably isn't interfering with my self-view or relationships, right?"

Be honest. Self-deception keeps us stuck. The truth will set us free.

Leave the line of communication open and respect what you see, and above all, trust that you can change anything you don't like.

Because you can.

Step 3: Make a plan

Now that you have—hopefully—done your homework, you should have a good sense of the condition of your four pillars, as well as which sledgehammer pillar breakers you're using to hurt your relationship with yourself.

That means the time has come to decide what you're going to do about it.

What pillar breakers are you going to train yourself out of? Which sledgehammers are you going to put down?

Which of your pillars need attention? If there's more than one, where do you want to start? Which self-care activities do you want to try to build that relationship? What are your goals for this relationship? What's the ideal vision you have for this partnership with yourself?

These are important questions to ask yourself, and only you have the answers.

It's okay if you look at that homework and feel overwhelmed. If you've got a lot of work to do, that's fantastic! That means you really can't go wrong here. Any change you make, however small, is bound to improve your situation.

It's like the target is so big that no matter where you throw the dart, you're going to get points.

All that matters now is that you begin.

Tips for Making This Relationship Last

Go slow.

You're not in a race here. There is no finish line when it comes to relationships. It's important to really let your new habits solidify before you move on so that treating yourself well just becomes second nature, and something you don't even have to think about. As annoying as it is, going slow allows for that level of integration.

For that reason, when you write your healing plan, make sure to break down your action steps into the tiniest steps possible. This will greatly increase your chances that the changes will stick.

Have realistic expectations for your transformation.

Pick one thing to work on. Just one. We don't want to run the risk of triggering overwhelm. You also don't need a six-page action plan to get going. Just one step. That's it. One. Something that you can do now.

For the love of all that's holy, be realistic. I know this is rich coming from someone who spends many hours of her life in fantasy worlds contemplating the *what ifs* of the universe, but yes, please be realistic. Don't expect that if you practice mental de-escalation for a week you'll suddenly become some kind of zen master who never gets angry again.

After all these years of self-work, I *still* get mad when I clean.

And I have a tendency to undertake changes with all the gusto of a baby rhino charging around, only to discover that I don't actually have my horn yet.

You have to grow into the new version of you. This takes time. This requires incremental change. If you wanted to grow basil, for example, from seed, you wouldn't bury the seed too deep in the soil or it would never reach the surface. You also wouldn't start pouring water on it and not stop until a plant appeared. We could have all the right ingredients and still miss the mark in our execution.

Everything grown must be done in moderation.

When you write out your plan, make sure your goals for yourself are SMART.

Very specific, very measurable (meaning you can track it), very achievable (doable), very relevant (it should be clear which pillar it connects to and what the purpose of the action is), and time bound, meaning give yourself a deadline and stick to it.

If I don't put things in my agenda, they don't happen. If I don't give tasks deadlines, they will hang in limbo for all time. I love to dillydally.

You can also add a progress check as part of your action plan. Decide when you're going to reevaluate your progress. Once a month? Once a quarter? Or once a year?

It may help to stop and check in like this because it's often difficult to see progress from moment to moment. Especially if we are moving slowly and thoroughly. It's usually only when I look back over time that I see the dramatic shifts I was hoping for.

Be consistent.

Don't forget that we're forming habits here. Unlearning "bad" ones and learning "good" ones. That's why I say it's better to start with small, easily repeatable actions that can become your new normal than to keep trying to take on more than you can handle, getting discouraged, and possibly giving up altogether.

Without repetition of the new desirable habits, you won't effectively replace the old habits. So make sure that your action steps in the plan are small enough to be repeatable every day.

A smaller step that you do every day will accumulate to more than a larger step that you can only manage once in a while. Another thing that makes consistency so important is that it really conveys that message of devotion.

If you were to say "That person is really devoted to me," you would be describing a person who is dependable. Someone who shows up day in and day out when they are needed. There's a correlation between consistency and dependability. You can learn to see yourself as a dependable person, specifically as someone *you* can depend on. This will help with your feelings of self-trust, one of the key components of our relationship with ourselves.

I have an unhelpful habit when it comes to forming habits. I tell myself that I will start on Monday. It seems like a natural placement considering that is the beginning of the week. Why not start something at the beginning of the week?

However, if I fall off the wagon, if I falter on, say, a Wednesday, or a Thursday, I'll tell myself that I'll start again on Monday.

You see the problem, don't you? I never establish the repetition needed to make a change permanent if I'm forever starting over on a Monday.

Don't wait for Monday.

Don't wait for anything. You could be dead tomorrow. At the very least, spend *one* day on yourself before you go.

Commit to beginning right now, wherever you are.

Don't wait for things to be perfect to begin, or you will never begin.

If you fall off the tightrope, commit to beginning again tomorrow at the latest. At the start of the next hour is better. If you make a mistake at 5:16, for example, tell yourself, "All right. That didn't work out. I'll start again at 6:00 p.m. I've got forty-five minutes to prepare."

Or sometimes I like to take a nap in the middle of the day, and when I wake up, I pretend like it's a new day and restart accordingly.

Be patient.

I am the most impatient person in the world, but I have high hopes for you. If you are also impatient, you'll be happy to know I still see progress in spite of my impatience. But it's also true that I never see progress as quickly as *I* want. Don't torture yourself like I do. If you're putting in the work each day, even if it's just five minutes of work, trust that it's adding up to something.

The alternative is to fall apart when you don't see a dramatic unveiling of your new life after three hours of meditation or journaling.

We won't see immediate and tremendous results. Anyone who promises you immediate and dramatic results is lying to you.

To protect yourself from discouragement, rely on its opposite: encouragement. Keep pumping yourself up as you go along. Be your own cheerful, endlessly optimistic Samwise. If you don't get this *Lord of the Rings* reference, I don't know where you've been.

But all you need to know in this context is that he's the best friend, the ride or die. And it's Sam's determination that proves critical to the success of the mission. He is often the one who encourages his friends to go on when all hope seems lost.

You're gonna have to carry the hope torch for yourself. You might even have to carry it for a long time.

I mean, I'm carrying it for you, too, but do I really have to do this by myself?

Patience teaches us how to delay gratification, which is hard because we live in an instant-gratification world.

We're used to getting what we want when we want it. This may not be true in all areas of our lives, but it's certainly truer than it was in the past. Eating junk food, retail therapy, especially online shopping, scrolling on social media, binging a series—all of this is instant gratification.

Instant gratification is problematic because it teaches us many bad habits. It weakens our self-control and our patience. Most long-term goals ask that we delay satisfaction and persevere. If we are not comfortable with the delayed nature of larger success, we will give up prematurely.

We can practice delaying gratification in small ways. Perhaps you love to turn on the TV as soon as you get home. Don't. Tell yourself you can turn it on in ten minutes. In twenty. In an hour. Same for picking up your phone and scrolling social media. Refrain for a few minutes and see how addicted you are to instant gratification.

Learning to build up resistance to the temptation of instant gratification will build self-discipline and patience. You may hate every minute of it now, but this tolerance will serve you well in life.

Track progress and celebrate milestones.

Don't leap into your next project or goal without celebrating your milestones. When we do this, we are continually telling ourselves that we aren't enough. For every goal we make, we move the goalpost further away. It compounds that sense of perpetual "not-enoughness" that we want to distance ourselves from.

Pause long enough to appreciate your victories, and to truly let them register. I am very guilty of immediately moving on to the next project. No sooner do I finish writing one book—an accomplishment—than I leap into the next. This creates a sense that the work is never done and that I myself am never getting far enough ahead.

It's a terrible feeling to cultivate. So don't.

Stop. Pause. Savor the results of your hard work.

Mark the moment however you like.

At the moment I have a fondness for caramel apples, so that's how I've been celebrating. But you must choose something that feels special to you.

Recommit as often as needed.

Shit happens, so sayeth the mystical bumper sticker. That will be true of your life as well. You'll get busy. You'll change jobs, change houses, change spouses—who knows. It is inevitable that even our best-laid plans may be interrupted. No matter the cause of the disruption, it is inevitable that we will falter in our self-discipline.

When we do, self-care is often the first thing we throw out the window as we adjust to our shifting circumstances.

It doesn't matter if you stumble. It doesn't even matter if, worse than a stumble, you fall flat on your face in a room full of cool people.

In fact, this is human.

It only matters that you keep recommitting to yourself and your well-being.

You're in this relationship for life, remember?

It's in difficult moments that we need ourselves the most. It's even more important to prioritize our self-care when tragedy strikes.

It is hard to resist the pressure to deprioritize ourselves at times like this. When all the alarm bells are going off and the kids are screaming, it can feel impossible to say, "I think I'll just take a little break right now."

But there is an element of self-discipline here. To keep committing to your care and well-being despite external pressure, that is discipline. That is *devotion*.

No matter what happens, no matter what is unfolding in your life, come back to yourself.

That's where your true power lies.

Make it part of your plan, deciding what you will do when you're disrupted. What's the first step you're going to take to reconnect with yourself?

Do you need to include self-check-ins on the calendar?

Do you need to have a weekly date with yourself? A coffee date that you won't miss no matter how busy you get?

Figure out what will work for you. What's the commitment you know you'll keep?

Use it to plan for disruption.

Plan for how you're going to begin again.

GRATITUDE

The key to lifelong wellness is having a great relationship with yourself. And the basis of any great relationship is gratitude. Or at least for me, it has been true that the best relationships in my life—the healthiest, most loving, strongest relationships—are the ones I'm deeply grateful for.

But how in the world do we become grateful for ourselves?

It certainly wasn't easy for me.

Thanksgiving is supposed to be *the* holiday of gratitude. But when I was fifteen, I remember clearly how much I despised it.

Kids from school were all excited for the break. And why not? They were getting a four-day weekend. They were looking forward to grand feasts full of their favorite foods. They were going to see their cousins and extended family which they hadn't seen for a while. They'd have time to hang out with their friends.

There was plenty to look forward to.

Not for me.

I had very different Thanksgiving plans that year. I was going down to the jailhouse to visit with my mother, who was serving time for her latest DUI.

While other kids were eating pie and watching football, I was walking into the jailhouse and getting patted down so I could go look at my mother through a pane of plexiglass. So that I could have an awkward, depressing conversation in which we both pretended to be okay and in decent spirits, when neither of us were.

At that moment, it was hard to be grateful when it felt like everyone else had it easier than I did.

Sometimes we hear the expression *gratitude practice*.

And I definitely had to practice. I had to practice at it *very* hard.

But over the years, I became great at gratitude. So good, in fact, that by the time my mother was murdered, I was skilled enough at practicing gratitude that I was able to find something to be grateful for even in losing her.

I wasn't grateful she was murdered, certainly not, but I was deeply grateful for the wisdom and release that came from the experience of losing her.

Within months of her death, I was able to recognize the embedded blessing in the experience.

Had my mother died peacefully in her sleep at the age of seventy or eighty, instead of tragically at fifty-six, I don't know that I would have discovered the truth about my family. Losing her as I did had left me with so much confusion that I'd been driven to understand what had happened. To make sense of her life and mine. To pursue truth relentlessly until I inadvertently uncovered family secrets long buried. And what I uncovered helped me to put all the remaining hurt between us to rest.

I understood my mother for the first time in my life.

I wouldn't have had the motivation to dig the way I had if she'd died any other way.

It was the very manner of my mother's death that presented an opportunity to receive the twin gifts of clarity and release.

I finally saw just how far I'd come as a person, and just how lucky I was to be alive.

I am grateful to myself today and who I've become.

And I hope you will be grateful for yourself too.

No matter how dark or difficult your past, no matter what has happened or will happen, you can get *really* good at gratitude with practice.

I want to close this book with a little activity to help you connect with this sense of gratitude for yourself. I think this will be the easiest way to show you what it feels like to love and appreciate yourself.

So if you would be so kind, indulge me for a few moments more.

I want you to think of something you're grateful for today. It could be your health. It could be your partner or your kids. After reading this book about broken families, maybe you're glad yours isn't so dysfunctional. Maybe it's getting your education, your job, chasing a dream, opening a business, getting your dog.

It can be anything, big or small. It just has to be something that makes you feel grateful.

Now envision the version of you who made that happen. Which version of you made the decision and took the actions that led you to acquire that which you are now grateful for.

Picture this version of you as clearly as you can.

For me, it would be the girl at the end of her grandmother's driveway. I can see her clearly in my head as she watches her mother walk back toward the house, a garbage bag full of her clothes in her hand. The girl who drove away crying, wondering if she's made the biggest mistake of her life, if she was in fact betraying the person she loved most in the world.

If I saw that girl on the street, I would run up to her and give her the biggest hug. I would thank her from the bottom of my heart for all that she did for me. For every choice, sacrifice, and tear.

If I'd tried to tell her how beautiful our life would become, she would have never believed me. She felt like the most worthless, incapable creature on the planet.

But I know better. *I* know who she really is and what she's capable of.

And I'm deeply grateful for her hard work and this life that she had the courage to create for me.

So which version of you are you grateful for?

Who gave you that which you view as most precious today?

Who gave you the health, the wealth, the happiness, the freedom, the chocolate donut of your dreams?

Picture them clearly in your mind, this past you. What are they wearing? What does their haircut look like? What kind of expression are they making as they see you walk up to them and scoop them up into a huge hug? Thank them with your whole heart for doing all that they've done for you.

How do they react when you thank them with your whole heart for doing all that they've done for you?

See this moment—this exchange between who you are and who you were—as clearly as you can. Sit with that feeling.

This is what it feels like to be grateful for yourself. To appreciate yourself. To be in a relationship with yourself.

Now there's a second part to this exercise. Because we can imagine not only the past but the future as well.

Imagine your dream life. Imagine this so-called better version of you that you're trying to create as we speak. That better life, that better you, that you're investing all your efforts into.

Imagine someone catches your eye on the street.

Their face lights up when they see you. They run up to you and squeeze you like you've saved their life.

Because you have.

After a moment of confusion, you realize that it's you. The future version of you that you're working so hard to manifest now is right here beaming at you like you're the person they've been searching for all along.

"Thank you," they say. "Thank you for everything you did for me. Everything I have now is because of you."

Feel what it feels like to be grateful for yourself.

Please sit with that.

Savor it.

Bask in it for as long as you can.

Please repeat this exercise as many times as you need to. Perhaps every day for the rest of your life, if that's what it takes to keep you moving forward.

Because this future version of you is not an illusion. This relationship you're building is not some dream.

This version of you knows what incredible, reality-defying magic you're capable of.

And so do I.

ENDNOTES

1. Stop Abuse Campaign. "Take Your ACE Test." https://stopabusecampaign.org/take-your-ace-test/. Accessed July 17, 2024.

2. University of Montana Center for Children, Families, and Workforce Development. "ACEs Factsheet." https://www.umt.edu/ccfwd/resource_library/physical-health/aces/acesfactsheet.pdf. Accessed July 17, 2024.

3. Afifi, Tracie O., et al. "Adverse Childhood Experiences and Physical Health Outcomes in Adulthood: Findings from a Nationally Representative Sample." *Journal of Child Psychology and Psychiatry*, vol. 61, no. 10, 2020, pp. 1049-1060. https://www.ncbi.nlm.nih.gov/pmc/articles/PMC7853397/. Accessed July 17, 2024.

4. The National Domestic Violence Hotline. "What Is Gaslighting?" https://www.thehotline.org/resources/what-is-gaslighting/. Accessed July 17, 2024.

5. McLean Hospital. "Teen Cutting and Self-Injury: Causes, Signs, and Treatment." https://www.mcleanhospital.org/essential/teen-cutting-and-self-injury. Accessed July 17, 2024.

6. Oxford English Dictionary. "Self-Care." https://www.oed.com/dictionary/self-care_n?tab=factsheet&tl=true#23790593. Accessed July 17, 2024.

7. Cleveland Clinic. "Emotional Dysregulation: Symptoms and Treatment." https://my.clevelandclinic.org/health/symptoms/25065-emotional-dysregulation. Accessed July 17, 2024.

8. Mayo Clinic. "Breaking Down Burnout in the Workplace." https://mcpress.mayoclinic.org/mental-health/breaking-down-burnout-in-the-workplace/. Accessed July 17, 2024.

ACKNOWLEDGMENTS

This book feels like it was a lifetime in the making.

How in the world could I possibly thank *everyone* who played a part? My wife, my friends, my dog, certainly—I'm blessed to have many people who add joy to my days. But for every dear one, there were ten or twenty who were kind in passing. Who shined their light, however briefly, on my grieving heart.

There are the podcast listeners who share their thoughts with me each week and help to guide this work. There's The World's Best Editor: Toby Selwyn.

There's my ever-enthusiastic critique group, The Four Horsemen of the Bookocalypse: Katie Pendleton, Angela Roquet, and Monica La Porta.

There's my street team. Thank you for reading the books in advance, reporting those lingering typos, and posting honest reviews. Your continued support means so much.

And then there's you, dear reader, who came this far with me, and you're still here even after the curtain has fallen. That's rather special, isn't it?

Thank you all for being here. You've made every struggle and dark moment worth it—just to be here with you now.

Thank you.

Thank you.

Thank you.

I hope you get everything you want from this life and more.

ALSO BY KORY M. SHRUM

Nonfiction

Who Killed My Mother? a memoir

Poetry (as K.B. Marie)

Birds & Other Dreamers

Questions for the Dead

You Can't Keep It

Fiction

Dying for a Living series

Dying for a Living

Dying by the Hour

Dying for Her: A Companion Novel

Dying Light

Worth Dying For

Dying Breath

Dying Day

Shadows in the Water series

Shadows in the Water

Under the Bones

Danse Macabre

Carnival

Devil's Luck

What Comes Around

Overkill

Silver Bullet

Hell House

One Foot in the Grave

Blood Rain

First Light

Castle Cove series

Welcome to Castle Cove

Night Tide

The City series

The City Below

The City Within

The City Outside

Other novels

Jack and the Fire Eater

Blade Born: A Borderlands Novel

Short Fiction

Thirst: new and collected stories

Final cut: stories

Learn more about Kory's work at: http://www.korymshrum.com/

ABOUT THE AUTHOR

Kory M. Shrum has enjoyed a prolific writing career, publishing over thirty books, including the bestselling *Shadows in the Water* and *Dying for a Living* series. Kory also expresses her creative spirit through poetry under the name K.B. Marie, showcasing her versatility as a writer.

She is the host of two podcasts, "Who Killed My Mother?", sharing the true story of her mother's tragic death, and A Well Cared For Human, a show focused on providing strategies and inspiration for investing in one's own wellbeing. You can listen to both for free on YouTube or your favorite podcast app.

Her commitment to mental health and environmental conservation is reflected in her philanthropic efforts, where she strives to make a meaningful impact, and when she's not working on her passion projects or creative work, Kory can usually be found under thick blankets with snacks. The kettle is almost always on.

She lives in Michigan with her equally bookish wife, Kim, and a very, *very* spoiled rescue dog, Max.

Learn more about Kory and her work at www.awellcaredforhuman.com or www.korymshrum.com.

www.ingramcontent.com/pod-product-compliance
Lightning Source LLC
Chambersburg PA
CBHW070056080526
44586CB00013B/1087